Praise for *LEAD NOW!*

"Solid, purposeful leadership is the cornerstone of any high-performing team. I have used the philosophy in *LEAD NOW!* and the many tools associated with it for myself and my leadership teams over numerous years—it's still as relevant today as it was on day one. Given the amount of quick, relatable material you can find, there are always copies of Stewart Leadership books on my desk to reference on a weekly basis."

DAVE CLARK chief financial officer, RSI

"*LEAD NOW!* and the leadership principles it subscribes to has been an essential resource for me and our organization. Whether you are leading a company or a group of ten to thousands of employees, this is a must-read and an invaluable tool for success."

MIKE KUSHIN president and CEO, BlackHorse Solutions

"*LEAD NOW!* is absolutely essential for all leaders everywhere! John Parker Stewart and Daniel J. Stewart's insight is fiercely accurate. Their advice and tips get right to the point on critical issues facing leaders today and provide no-nonsense guidance to steer through very difficult times."

DAVID J. DACQUINO chairman and CEO, Serco Inc.

"As a firm believer and follower of the LEAD NOW! Model, I couldn't be more excited about this second edition. I have always enjoyed the simple and balanced approach that this model used. Being a busy executive, I researched several other models but found that they always seemed to make it harder than it had to be. The action tips and planning in *LEAD NOW!* were always my favorite, and I'm not sure how, but they have added even more content and examples. The key to success is in the personal change section, and John Parker Stewart and Daniel J. Stewart have once again found a way to connect on a deeper and more meaningful level. A must-read for leaders wanting more!"

TINA M. SEMOTAN chief administration officer, Franklin Energy and AM Conservation Group

"Thank goodness John Parker Stewart and Daniel J. Stewart have put these updated coaching tips in print! Now I can get rid of all the crib notes I have jotted down from conversations with them as I faced new or rapidly changing leadership challenges. This isn't another management book. It is a compilation of the right things John and Daniel have observed leaders do over the forty-plus years they have worked with leaders and in leadership development. I wouldn't go into bear country without a gun. I certainly won't go into the boardroom without *LEAD NOW!*. Thank you, John and Daniel—truly world-class coaches!"

KEN ASBURY former president and CEO, CACI

"*LEAD NOW!* is a must-read for all leaders! Over the past twenty-plus years, John's books and coaching have helped me understand what it takes and means to be a leader. John Parker Stewart and Daniel J. Stewart's writing style is clear, concise, and profound. I have read and reread their books and always find another leadership gem. John has been a personal and corporate coach for me and my company, and his books have been an important part of the experience. They've enabled me, in the quiet of the day, to reflect on and learn from my past decisions."

DAN HEIMERDINGER CEO, Exostrategies, Inc.

"In the crowded space of leadership development professionals, there are two voices I trust for inspiration, integrity, and easily learned and implemented skills sets: John Parker Stewart and Daniel J. Stewart. This is *the* book you need right now to refine your personal and professional leadership skills and take your business to the next level. *LEAD NOW!* outlines exactly how to develop personal and professional skill sets to make you and your business highly successful. Read, apply, and experience the difference."

RICHARD B. EVANS CEO, Health Care Solutions International

"The *LEAD NOW!* book provides a proven and practical approach to elevating leaders. It focuses leaders on what they need to do right now to develop themselves. It acts as a trusted field guide to which leaders can return time and again for what they need to work on next. Use it to develop your leadership and see the difference!"

THOMAS E. KNOTHE JD, board chair and interim CEO, Marine Credit Union; associate professor and dean emeritus, College of Business, Performing Arts, and Leadership, Viterbo University

"The single most important asset that drives a successful business is the strength of its leadership. *LEAD NOW!* provides an action-oriented change management plan for improving your leadership skills. Implementation of this book will result in improved strategic planning, program performance, customer satisfaction, and personal development. John Parker Stewart and Daniel J. Stewart capture and apply their decades of experience in coaching and organizational development in a book that provides a can-do method to help you evolve your leadership skills. I endorse this book and believe it is one that every leader should use for practical application of leadership techniques."

CAREY A. SMITH former president, Honeywell Technology Solutions Inc.

"*LEAD NOW!* is a must-read for any leader who wants to grow. By breaking down the essentials of successful leadership into easy-to-apply tips, *LEAD NOW!* has given me tools that are critical to leading a group of people to be the best that they can be... which is what leadership is all about!"

TINA DOLPH president and CEO, Siemens Government Technologies

"I highly recommend *LEAD NOW!*. Stewart Leadership is the best I have encountered to lead an organization through the process of improving the skills of its leaders. John Parker Stewart and Daniel J. Stewart's techniques work! My teams and I have benefited from Stewart Leadership's guidance many times over the past fifteen years. Grasp the coaching tips in *LEAD NOW!* and you will be a better person, and a better leader. I use them every day."

JAY F. HONEYCUTT former center director (CEO), Kennedy Space Center; former president, Lockheed Martin Space Operations

"I have used the trio of Stewart Leadership books (*LEAD NOW!*, *52 Leadership Lessons*, and *52 Leadership Gems*) in combination with coaching to successfully develop leaders and teams. Since it's packed with an additional ten years' worth of key learnings, I can't wait to apply the latest insights in this second edition of *LEAD NOW!* with my leaders today!"

LORI WIGHTMAN RN, DNP, NEA-BC; SVP and chief nursing officer, SCL Health

"Stewart Leadership is a one-of-a-kind provider in building great company cultures. It's founder, John Parker Stewart, has a deep and empathetic sense of people's needs, desires, and goals. His perspective on how teams can best work together is unusually perceptive. John's commitment is also partner-oriented. He becomes a key member of the teams he is advising, and the team members trust him as a result and view him as a member of their group. All of this knowledge and perspective is encapsulated in *LEAD NOW!*—essential reading for all leaders to be their best selves and get their team members to achieve top performance!"

MAC LAFOLLETTE founder, The GC Companies; chairman, Valiant Integrated Services; chairman, AVANTech

"With *LEAD NOW!*, John Parker Stewart and Daniel J. Stewart make the complex simple and the difficult actionable. Their coaching tips and action-planning approach enable a leader at any level to successfully lead their team and engage their people in today's changing workplace."

ANDREW GREENWOOD director of corporate marketing and communications, ZS Associates

"The Stewarts' LEAD NOW! Leadership Development Model is a superb framework for all true leaders to follow. Not only is it based on experience and demonstrated performance, it also capitalizes on lessons learned in real-world situations, cutting across a variety of prominent corporations and government agencies as well. Whether you're a seasoned professional or new to leadership responsibilities, LEAD NOW! is sure to inspire!"

DON FULOP former EVP for business development, CACI

"LEAD NOW! provides an action-oriented and clear plan for improving your leadership skills. Implementation of the plan will result in improved strategic planning, organizational performance, customer satisfaction, and personal development. You will lead better, be more productive, and have a more effective organization. I highly endorse LEAD NOW! to take your leaders to the next level!"

LYNN DUGLE former CEO and chairman of the board, Engility; current Fortune 200 board director

"Stewart Leadership has provided a leadership blueprint that will drastically improve any leader's capabilities. Their forty-plus years of experience working with leaders in both the public and private sectors is on full display in this book. My teams and I have benefited greatly from the experiences and teachings in LEAD NOW!. The process and techniques in this book will transform any organization. This is a must-read for any leader who is looking to build their leadership capacity!"

DAN CORBETT CEO, Valiant Integrated Services

"The art of leadership requires great communication, strategic analysis and direction, and clear accountability. In *LEAD NOW!*, John Parker Stewart and Daniel J. Stewart bring it all together in a practical, easy-to-access, actionable package that is a must-read for anyone who wants to master the art of great leadership!"

RACHELE LEHR SVP of human resources and administration, Briggs & Stratton

"*LEAD NOW!* is an accessible leadership reference guide full of time-tested insights, practical how-to advice, and easy-to-use tools that allow readers to quickly build personalized action plans for sustained change. It will become an indispensable handbook for both those new to leadership and seasoned veterans alike."

DAVE KIEVET president, The Boldt Company

"John Parker Stewart and Daniel J. Stewart capture and apply their decades of experience in coaching and organizational development in a book that provides a can-do method to help you evolve your leadership skills. I endorse this book and believe it is one every leader should use for practical application of leadership techniques."

MARCELO PODESTA president, National Business Furniture

"*LEAD NOW!* is my indispensable guide for developing new and experienced leaders. There are hundreds of tips and keys inside that help program managers lead teams. John Parker Stewart and Daniel J. Stewart are truly world-class coaches, who have compiled a complete guide to successful leadership at all levels!"

MICHAEL MILLANE principal program manager, Intel Corporation

"I heartily endorse *LEAD NOW!*. I have greatly benefited from Stewart Leadership's insightful and practical leadership teachings. Their vast experience, positive energy, and passion for developing leaders at all levels create common-sense concepts and solutions that can directly and easily be applied to both personal and professional leadership challenges."

MICHAEL A. DIGNAM former president and CEO, PAE; current CEO, CRDF Global

"It has been my pleasure working with John Parker Stewart and Daniel J. Stewart over this past decade. Their coaching techniques and ability to quickly build trust with teams and individual leaders is outstanding. They are truly making a difference and are why *LEAD NOW!* has been a part of my leadership curriculum for many years."

SUSAN BALAGUER chief human resources officer, Parsons Corporation

"I am privileged to endorse *LEAD NOW!* as the go-to guide for anyone who claims to be a leader. I have had the honor of working with John Parker Stewart on integral problem-solving at the leadership level, coupled with an inspirational improvement that really hits home with senior leadership. John is a passionate coach who makes the complex simple and difficult tasks obtainable. I highly endorse this easy-to-apply leadership guide, which all potential and current leaders need."

LARRY MCGILL chairman, KanPak–Golden State Foods

"The second edition of *LEAD NOW!* is packed with guidelines, development tips, and plans for any leader who needs an approach to motivate team members, build and maintain relationships, and achieve high performance. *LEAD NOW!* provides the tools for managers, mentors, and coaches to develop individuals and teams while also giving individual employees an opportunity to self-direct their development. It reminds me of a smarter version of FYI. The book is a winner!"

TOM MCMAHON former EVP, chief sales and merchandising officer, Grocery Outlet

"*LEAD NOW!* is my go-to resource for coaching tips, mentoring sessions, and complicated leadership development discussions. John Parker Stewart and Daniel J. Stewart have developed a set of quick tips and answers that almost rivals them being with you in person. Their 21 Leadership Dimensions provide a comprehensive way to organize your talent management program from performance reviews all the way through succession planning. Bravo to John and Daniel for developing such an effective and practical way to reinforce good leadership!"

PAUL A. DILLAHAY president and CEO, NCI

"Stewart Leadership has been a guiding team for me for many years, and they continue to find new ways to help me and many others grow in our fields. We all have too much noise in today's world and *LEAD NOW!* provides the noise canceling that is needed to focus on what is truly important for you, your teams, and your company. Seldom do leaders find a book (and program) that is directly applicable to the day to day like *LEAD NOW!*"

DAN COX CEO, Clinical Education Alliance

"I recommend *LEAD NOW!* for leaders to grow their scale of impact and results; expand their depth, breadth, and effectiveness of relationships across functions and with customers; and to build teaming cultures to effectively drive change. The LEAD NOW! framework is comprehensive across essential leadership dimensions, simple in presentation, and profound when applied. The LEAD NOW! approach also includes ongoing learning to continually enhance your leadership skills. You will find both immediate effect and ongoing improvements as you reference the book over time."

MATT MACCONNEL VP of customer excellence, Ansys

"Connecting with Stewart Leadership was my key to successfully transforming the National Agricultural Statistics Service of the USDA in how, where, and what it did to produce enhanced products more cost effectively. By following the steps outlined in *LEAD NOW!*, my team led a business and cultural transformation that brought meaningful purpose for the staff, delivered excellence in the agency's products, and developed leadership and staff expertise. This effort resulted in more timely and more reliable agricultural statistics with enhanced user satisfaction at a reduced cost."

CYNTHIA Z.F. CLARK former administrator, National Agricultural Statistics Service, USDA

"*LEAD NOW!* is a must-have resource for today's business leader. What Stewart Leadership has achieved is the most practical collection of tools for today's business challenges that can easily be applied for immediate impact. I use *LEAD NOW!* as my go-to reference more than any other leadership resource out there."

CARIN CASSO REINHARDT chief people officer, NewAge, Inc.

"Since first being exposed to this series with training by John Parker Stewart, *LEAD NOW!* has become an essential resource for me as I have transitioned through leadership roles. Understanding the 21 Leadership Dimensions and using them to understand and motivate both myself and my staff has been a key element in our success. I can always find a relevant leadership tip for each crisis!"

SCOTT "SCOOTER" ALTMAN president of Operating Group Space, ASRC Federal; former NASA shuttle commander

LEAD NOW!

Other books in the Stewart Leadership Series

52 Leadership Gems:
Practical and Quick Insights for Leading Others

52 Leadership Lessons:
Timeless Stories for the Modern Leader

JOHN PARKER STEWART
DANIEL J. STEWART

SECOND EDITION • NEWLY REVISED

LEAD NOW!

A Personal Leadership Coaching Guide for Results-Driven Leaders

Cataloguing in publication information is
available from Library and Archives Canada.
ISBN 978-1-77458-193-3 (paperback)
ISBN 978-1-77458-194-0 (ebook)

Page Two
pagetwo.com

Edited by James Harbeck
Copyedited by Steph VanderMeulen
Proofread by Alison Strobel
Cover design by Peter Cocking
Interior design and illustrations by Setareh Ashrafologhalai

stewartleadership.com

We dedicate this book to the thousands of leaders we have coached over the past decades. You have come to us from every country and every industry with challenges that cover the spectrum of managerial life. Your desire to learn, progress, and succeed has been a driving force in our lives. We salute you!

Contents

Introduction

AMERICAN BUSINESSMAN and religious leader M. Russell Ballard shares the following profound story in the May 2011 issue of *Ensign* magazine: There was once a young merchant who wanted to strike it rich during the California gold rush of 1849. He sold his Boston-based store, packed up everything he owned, and headed across the country to make his fortune.

One day, after unsuccessfully panning for gold over several months, an old prospector came by and asked the young man how it was going. With great frustration, the young man explained that he had so little to show for his efforts. He pointed to the large pouch hanging from the prospector's belt and stated, "I want to find big nuggets of gold like what you have in your pouch! All I'm finding are small bits of gold."

The old prospector smiled and responded, "You think I have large nuggets, do you? You think that is the goal?" And with a steady motion, the prospector took the pouch off his belt and turned it upside down. Out fell a thousand small flecks of gold. There was not one large nugget! The prospector's success came in the careful collection of the small pieces of gold, which added up to great wealth.

In coaching thousands of leaders, it is our experience that too often, leaders are looking for a single experience that will vault them to success—the unique moment that qualifies them as a complete leader. But like the Boston merchant, they misunderstand how true leadership is created. Real and lasting improvements in one's skill level and leadership talents are developed one small step at a time. From small and simple things, major gains occur.

The great founder of Marriott International, J. Willard Marriott, expressed his personal philosophy of management: "You can't improve 1,000 percent in one thing, but you can improve 1 percent in a thousand things." Over the course of his successful career, Mr. Marriott learned the same lesson the old prospector had, that it takes many small "flecks" patiently yet persistently acquired over time to add up to the desired level of performance.

The same is true in one's desire to become a solid and trusted leader—whether in industry, teaching, business, community, parenting, church, school, coaching, medicine, law, science, art, music, military, athletics, or any endeavor. It is unrealistic to expect large, major leaps of progress overnight. The truth is that it takes persistent, patient effort over time to see and experience gains in one's ability to lead—one fleck at a time.

LEAD NOW! was created to help leaders develop the tools to identify and improve their ability to lead and coach others at a moment's notice. This book is filled with hundreds of small golden flecks—called tips—divided across twenty-one Leadership Dimensions that are designed to help any leader in any field grow in their ability to lead more effectively—one "fleck" at a time.

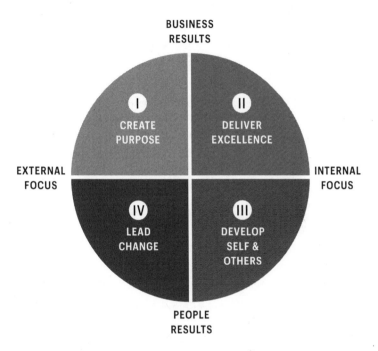

This book came about as a result of our years of observing extremely busy leaders. Most leaders want to improve but can barely find the time to manage everything they are already doing. Our motivation in developing the LEAD NOW! concept was to produce a model that is practical, useful, easy to teach, easy to understand, and that smacks of common sense. The LEAD NOW! Leadership Development Model gives leaders at all levels a simple and comprehensive framework for the critical areas of leading others.

The content for LEAD NOW! draws on two sources: 1) the authors' extensive organizational consulting and coaching experience, and 2) proprietary 360-degree and team effectiveness assessments performed over the last four decades.

Clients have included organizations and leaders from a host of government agencies, Fortune 500 companies, healthcare, manufacturing, financial services, and government contractors in the aerospace, defense, technology, energy, electronics, software, and communications industries. Combining this professional experience with industry best practices and academic research, the LEAD NOW! Model offers a solid foundation for busy leaders to build and refine their skills as they practice the art of being a leader in today's changing environment.

This model is built on the assumption that leaders must achieve aligned and positive results from four perspectives: 1) their people, 2) their business, 3) their marketplace (external), and 4) their organization (internal).

These four points of view become the two axes that encompass the four areas of great leadership: Create Purpose, Deliver Excellence, Develop Self & Others, and Lead Change. Each of these four quadrants is supported by several key Leadership Dimensions and provides the basis for in-depth leadership development action planning.

Leadership is critical to an organization's performance, and leaders become better through focused and supported development. The LEAD NOW! Leadership Development Model provides the foundation for any personalized leadership development effort, whether it is a coaching engagement, a workshop, or a larger leadership program. Using the LEAD NOW! Model will help you identify and improve the behaviors needed to increase your success in leading others and achieving desired organizational results.

Becoming an agile, flexible leader requires easily accessible leadership development tools. *LEAD NOW!* provides a user-friendly and complete action guide for leaders at every level of the organization. In fact, this book was not written to be read—it was written to be *used*! As you dive into this book, select a Leadership Dimension to focus on, take some of the tips and ideas into an action plan, and shut the book and go to work! We created this book so you can quickly put these ideas into practice and strengthen your leadership ability every day.

This *LEAD NOW!* book consists of three parts:

Part I: Introducing the LEAD NOW! Leadership Development Model lays out the foundations of the model, discusses the four critical relationships for any leader, and shows how to turn insights from this book into action.

Part II: The 21 Dimensions dedicates a chapter to each Leadership Dimension. Each chapter teaches you what it looks like when that Dimension is done successfully and when it is overused, and gives you scores of actionable tips—flecks of gold to enrich your leadership. At the end of each Dimension is a self-assessment with key questions to help you reflect on your current leadership skills and attitudes.

Part III: Assessing and Planning helps you see where you stand and decide where you're going. There are three options for assessing your current abilities, followed by a detailed action plan template with guidelines on how to set your goals. At the end of the book, we have included a blank action plan and two filled-in sample action plans to help you get started on making your own effective goal statements and focus areas.

Several assumptions and beliefs form the foundation for *LEAD NOW!*:

* Leadership is critical to an organization's performance.

* Leaders can and should be developed.

- Organizations benefit by investing in developing and retaining good leaders.

- Leadership development requires significant, specific, and focused effort.

- Development without support and follow-up produces little to no change.

Leadership is a future-oriented ability to establish direction, align people, and help others to work together. We believe a leader is one who develops a vision of the future, prepares the strategies for achieving it, and supports the execution of that vision.

We also strongly believe that the ability to develop and execute the what and how of vision resides in basic leadership behaviors. Identifying and improving these specific behaviors will increase the success of leading.

In the first edition of this book, we introduced and developed the concepts. In this revised second edition, we are proud to provide a complete handbook for achieving the results you desire and that you are responsible for, with even more insights and tools to support you on your leadership journey. From additional and updated tips, research, and explanations, this next generation of *LEAD NOW!* will no doubt elevate and inspire you even more. We are excited and honored to be a part of your leadership journey with you!

PART I

INTRODUCING THE LEAD NOW! LEADERSHIP DEVELOPMENT MODEL

Leadership
as a Journey

ONE OF our wonderful colleagues, John Zorbini, often said that if leadership were a car, you would think it must be a classic red Ferrari with the way we traditionally talk about it—or even the way we all think to ourselves about it. We sometimes put the idea of leadership on a pedestal and speak about it reverently. It's the idea that when you become a leader, you are blessed with instant knowledge, judgment, and prestige.

But, Zorbini pointed out, if leadership really were a car, it would be a beat-up old truck. It would have dents and dings. Maybe the side panels would be different colors and the interior worn out, but it would have four wheels, move, and get the job done. It's functional but not glamorous, and the messiness of learning to lead is visible.

People often work very hard to earn that glorious, vaunted leadership position. These people are often skilled, driven, and ambitious. They have striven throughout their career to advance, achieve, and gain influence, and once they get into the chair, they feel as though they have "arrived." It comes from the idea that once you become a leader, you have achieved your goals—you have reached the pinnacle of your career and now you can reap the rewards.

What we have learned from watching leaders struggle at all levels is this: leadership is a privilege and, to some, a calling. It is a craft, a set of unique skills that requires dedicated practice, and is more of a journey than a destination. Intelligence, past successes, or tenure do not ensure success. Leadership responsibilities require new skills and mindsets to be successful, and these new skills rarely develop spontaneously—instead, leadership skills must, and can, be learned.

Whether you are just starting out as a leader or have put years into the effort, effective leadership is something you learn as you go along. At every stage of our leadership journey, we are called upon to use a skill we just learned or haven't yet mastered. We will make mistakes along the way, and there will be moments that remind us to be humble. What makes these moments worth it is that leadership can be deeply fulfilling and rewarding. Your organization and your team need great leaders, and positioning you with the right tools and expectations is what this book is all about.

Leadership Is an Art

> "Learn the rules like a pro, so
> you can break them like an artist."
>
> PABLO PICASSO

One of the best, and worst, things about the study and practice of leadership that it is a never-ending skill set to master. There will never be a single moment in which your mastery of the subject will become absolute.

And this is largely a result of the complexity and diversity of human experience. While we can improve ourselves and continually work toward a level of proficiency in each Leadership Dimension, the art of leadership requires knowing which tools to use in any given situation and how to wield them at that moment.

Everyone has a distinct approach to leadership. It's incredibly personal and there is no one-size-fits-all solution. To each Leadership Dimension, you will bring a different set of strengths from anyone else. This means that you must develop your leadership style using the building blocks of the 21 Leadership Dimensions and your understanding of the quadrants and relationships they connect to.

This lack of a clear answer or direction can be frustrating for those of us who prefer things to be more black and white. Leaders must learn to be comfortable with a sense of ambiguity. While leadership is work in and of itself, it isn't a spreadsheet into which we can type our inputs for clean calculations and even, consistent results. Leadership is messier than we want it to be.

Leadership Is Personal

But it is this "messiness" that liberates you as a leader. It means that there is nothing you need to succeed that you do not already have within you. Effective leadership must come from an authentic place, and leaders cannot all act the same, because we are not all the same.

Adding to the overall complexity is that leaders must leverage not only their own strengths, but also the strengths of others. This means that every person you lead will require different things from you at different times, and your approach must be personalized to each person, each outcome, and each solution.

The leadership style you develop will be uniquely your own and you will want others to see you this way, to understand your strengths as a leader and the value you provide. Part of achieving that recognition as a leader are the skill and willingness with which you use that same lens for others.

The LEAD NOW! Model and approach to leadership development will support you as you develop your leadership style because there is no prescriptive element for each Dimension. This book provides quotes, tips, resource references, and self-assessment questions for each Leadership Dimension.

The LEAD NOW! Leadership Development Model

THE AWARD-WINNING LEAD NOW! Model has been developed over forty-five years of research and professional consulting and coaching experience. It has its roots in over eight thousand 360-degree assessments measuring leadership effectiveness at all levels of organizations and across dozens of industries, nonprofits, and government organizations. It also draws from thousands of interviews with leaders to distill what great leadership is all about.

The LEAD NOW! Leadership Development Model was created to provide leaders with a simple and comprehensive framework for the critical areas of leading others. It is a results-oriented model geared toward achieving results in both business and people, focusing on reaching excellence within the organization, and understanding the competitive marketplace and customer needs outside the organization.

Roots of the LEAD NOW! Model

Over the years, there have been many ways to understand, describe, theorize, and develop leadership. The LEAD NOW! Model stands on the shoulders of so many great thinkers and practitioners, as each has sought to explain what makes and is a great leader.

The Great Man and Trait Theories

Some of the earliest ways of understanding who a leader is and how a leader is chosen involve natural-born traits. Traditionally, taller, stronger, or more decisive individuals, too often only men, have been seen as more leader-like—as have louder, more extroverted, and more self-confident people. This view also assumes that once a person becomes a leader, their power, knowledge, and wisdom instantly increase and vault them into a higher realm of glory and perspective.

While we acknowledge that these characteristics have in many cases been a significant reason individuals are looked upon as leaders, we assert with the strongest voice that this view is filled with dangerous bias, has caused great harm to so many over the years, and has fueled many debilitating myths. The tallest, fastest, or strongest does not automatically make the best leader, nor does becoming a leader instantly grant omniscience. We reject and fight against the beliefs that the leader does or should know everything, should only be a man, and is only determined by inborn and untrainable attributes. LEAD NOW! is centered on the belief that everyone has the potential to develop themselves along their leadership journey, and that no one is above the need for continued development regardless of where or how they start.

Situational and Contingency Theories

In contrast to the traits view of leadership, the situational perspective acknowledges that there is no one right way of leading. Instead, the best leader assesses the situation and adjusts their style and response based on the people, tasks, and desired results. In other words, there are many right ways of leading others contingent upon the competence, confidence, and context of the situation.

The LEAD NOW! Model advocates the need for leaders to consider the situation and adjust their leadership response accordingly. While there are many important leadership behaviors, the best leaders are able to build leadership muscle in each area and have the wisdom to know when and how to flex that muscle. Leaders can be aware of their own styles, the styles and needs of others, and the needs of the situation to balance and adjust their responses.

Management and Behavior Theories

The behavioral perspective believes that leaders act in a system of rewards or punishments and that their behavior both works within and reinforces these consequences. However, it also suggests that the leader's behaviors can impact, shift, and change these systems and the people they lead. It is based on a belief that within any transaction with others, leaders learn through teaching, observation, and doing and become better as they practice their leadership abilities, and their people benefit from their leader's ongoing development.

The actions of leaders matter, and the LEAD NOW! Model is built on the belief that leaders can and should continually learn and improve. People are better served when leaders recognize their impact on others, how organizational systems and processes influence them and how they make decisions, and how they can shape and support the culture in positive ways. When leaders prioritize their own learning as well as the development of their people, they can get better business and people results.

Relationship and Participative Theories

One of the newer ways of explaining leadership is based on the human connection of leader and follower. These theories describe the best leader as focusing on building a strong relationship with others, seeing the higher good from the task, empowering each person in their potential and performance, and actively seeking insight from others. At its foundation, this perspective values people holistically and not as objects or resources to accomplish tasks. It supports the leader holding the decision-making rights while encouraging active participation from everyone. The leader's responsibility is more than getting the job done; it is all about helping people feel fulfilled at work and looking at work as one part of their life.

The LEAD NOW! Model is centered on building great relationships; identifying the strengths, challenges, and pressures of others; and actively building close ties of trust and engagement with each person. A leader has a high responsibility to treat others with dignity and respect, to act with integrity and an inclusive mindset, and to leverage and develop the talents and skills of others to accomplish aligned business and people results.

How the Model Works

A great quality of the LEAD NOW! Model is how many ways it can guide, develop, and benefit leaders and organizations.

It is a multifaceted model that brings tremendous depth while still explaining leadership in a practical and easy-to-apply way.

The most important aspect of being a leader is achieving results—business results *and* people results. Business results are all about financial, budgetary, and operational success; people results are about team dynamics, workforce engagement, the overall employee experience, career development, and feeling connected with each other. Too often, we focus only on business results; our research has found that a great leader needs to be able to achieve both kinds of results—the IQ-driven side of creating purpose and delivering excellence, and the EQ-driven side of developing self and others and leading change. You have to know how to achieve the numbers *and* how to speak the language.

The LEAD NOW! Leadership Development Model helps clarify the expectations for a complete leader in terms of results and relationships:

- **Business results** means being able to achieve operational success. This is the language of the boss; the leader needs to be able to speak that language well to build the relationship with the boss for success.

- **People results** means being able to achieve success within your team engagement development. This is the language of your direct reports; they are most interested in engagement, development, and interaction with others on the team.

- **Internal focus** means being able to accomplish internal excellence. This is the language of your peers; they care most about the process handoff points between you and others—fairness of resource allocation, the level of quality that they should be expecting, and roles and responsibilities.

- **External focus** means understanding the voice of the customer—understanding their needs and knowing their needs even before they do. This is the language of your customers; they care most about having their needs understood. They will ask questions like, "Do you know what I need, even before I do?" and "Do you understand the alternatives that I have in the marketplace, the competitive landscape, and how you're interpreting that to add value more to me?"

The four quadrants created by the interaction of these axes describe the expectations of what a great leader needs to do: create purpose, deliver excellence, develop self and others, and lead change. The 21 Leadership Dimensions within the quadrants are a buffet of different skills or competencies that a leader can then choose from to help develop themselves as a leader. The ultimate goal of the LEAD NOW! Model is to develop leadership muscle in all four of these quadrants—and especially in the people-focused side—to enable leaders to not only get a seat at the leadership table, but also remain there.

The model also helps explain when and how people typically get promoted. Usually people get promoted because they are great delivering excellence—the intersection of business results and internal focus. They are technically gifted individual contributors. As they begin their leadership journey, they must begin to embrace a new skill set—the leadership skill set. They turn their internal focus toward people and build the ability to develop themselves and others.

On the basis of that, they learn more about leading change, influence, and introducing new ideas as they turn toward developing their external focus. As they continue to communicate more effectively, they learn to think more strategically about business results and to create and reinforce purpose. Finally, they complete the circle when they are able to make decisions, problem-solve, and delegate to deliver excellence at a higher level. The new manager is no longer just getting work done through themselves, but getting work done with and through others.

The Quadrants and Dimensions

Our LEAD NOW! Model is composed of four quadrants, each supported by several key Leadership Dimensions. These are specific leadership skills and behaviors that have been grouped according to the goal identified by each quadrant. These behaviors are the elements of leadership, the building

blocks that we stack together in order to rise to the occasion and succeed as leaders. These Dimensions provide the basis for in-depth leadership development action planning.

Quadrant I: Create Purpose

Externally Focused Business Results

As a leader, you must be responsible for defining vision and strategy. Quadrant I, Create Purpose, identifies what the organization stands for, what it is going to do, and how it is positioned in the marketplace. It identifies the vision, addresses what need is being satisfied, and why we are doing it. This involves:

- Communicating effectively with others
- Knowing the competition
- Understanding the customer
- Analyzing marketplace trends
- Setting strategy

Quadrant I includes these Leadership Dimensions:

1 **Customer Focus.** Delivering your product or service in such a way that you fulfill the needs, wants, and values of your customer better than anyone else.

2 **Effective Communication.** Expressing an intended message, through the correct medium, in a manner that the recipient of the message will understand.

3 **Presentation Skills.** Effectively communicating ideas to large or small audiences.

4 **Strategic Thinking.** Balancing short- and long-term actions to optimize business results.

Quadrant II: Deliver Excellence

Internally Focused Business Results

As a leader, you are responsible for delivering operational excellence—translating the strategy into day-to-day execution for the organization. Quadrant II, Deliver Excellence, is ensuring that metrics are clear and deliverables are accomplished. This involves:

- Building consistent and measurable processes
- Clear decision making
- Delivering operational results
- Continuous improvement
- Behaving with integrity

Quadrant II includes these Leadership Dimensions:

5 **Decision Making.** Understanding not only why a decision needs to be made, but also the vital steps of defining and analyzing the problem, followed by reaching and implementing the decision, all while communicating openly to those who will be affected by the outcome.

6 **Delegating.** Communicating a given task so that the individual assigned understands the objective and timeline, is provided available resources to complete the task, and knows you will support them without taking over the task.

7 **Dependability.** Receiving an assignment and consistently following through and delivering the expected results.

8 **Focusing on Results.** Focusing on the desired outcome with precision and conviction.

9 **Personal Integrity.** Demonstrating consistent honesty and commitment to your word.

10 **Problem Solving.** Defining and analyzing a problem that leads to a high-quality solution with appropriate buy-in.

Quadrant III: Develop Self & Others

Internally Focused People Results

As a leader, you must value learning for yourself and for others. Quadrant III, Develop Self & Others, is ensuring you spend time building the talent on your team, coaching others effectively, and staying current on the advances in your profession and industry.

This involves:

- Personal improvement opportunities
- Building and managing team dynamics
- Honing technical expertise
- Coaching and developing others
- Managing one's ego

Quadrant III includes these Leadership Dimensions:

11 **Coaching.** Guiding an individual to achieve improved performance through self-discovery, feedback, encouragement, and skill development.

12 **Ego Management.** Creating a balanced level of confidence in your own skills, tools, judgment, and experience.

13 **Listening.** Understanding the intended message while having an awareness of the attitudes and feelings of others.

14 **Personal Development.** Continuously pursuing improvement in your abilities and knowledge.

15 **Team Building.** Helping a group of individuals work together to accomplish a common goal.

16 **Time Management.** Planning and controlling how you spend the hours in your day to effectively accomplish your goals and meet deadlines.

17 **Valuing Others.** Recognizing the potential within others and letting them know that their capabilities, experience, and contributions are important.

Quadrant IV: Lead Change

Externally Focused People Results

As a leader, you are responsible for creating and championing change efforts that will benefit the organization. Quadrant IV, Lead Change, is understanding the broader marketplace and developing the engagement of others to create united and sustainable growth.

This involves:

- Influencing key decision makers
- Sponsoring change projects
- Empowering stakeholders
- Encouraging innovation
- Managing resistance

Quadrant IV includes these Leadership Dimensions:

18 **Change Management.** Communicating a compelling vision, leading minor and major changes within an organization, and sustaining the change over time.

19 **Innovation.** Applying better solutions to current or future needs.

20 **Inspiring Commitment.** Earning the hearts and minds of those with whom you associate.

21 **Organizational Savvy.** Knowing how to get things done through formal and informal channels.

The Four Critical Relationships All Leaders Must Develop

HAVE YOU ever considered how often we adjust our communication topics and frequency based on the relationships we have? Our partners or spouses may typically want frequent, highly specific check-ins; our teenagers may want the minimum acceptable level of communication; our parents may like us to call weekly or monthly with some general updates about the family; and our friends could be OK with whatever communication happens within our busy life.

At work, leaders have four critical relationships they must develop and within which they must communicate appropriately: with the boss, direct reports, peers, and customers. Each relationship is essential and deserves focused attention, but each relationship values and needs different things to be productive. And yet, unlike in our personal relationships, we can sometimes fall into the trap of treating each business relationship in the same way—neglecting the unique needs of each and not respecting what each considers necessary.

It is an easy mistake to make, as we treat others based more on our needs than theirs. However, understanding and adjusting to the specific needs of each of these four types of relationships is critical for a leader to be successful.

So, what are the individual needs for each critical relationship? What are the languages, values, and ways to strengthen each relationship? Effective leadership requires that each of the four relationships receives the time, attention, and messages valued the most.

Using the LEAD NOW! Leadership Development Model as a framework, we can identify what each critical relationship cares about most to help avoid relationship-poor leadership. Each relationship speaks a different language, explained below:

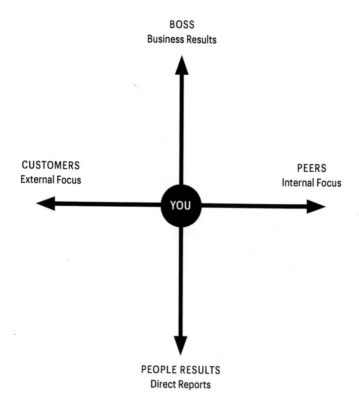

Boss

To build an effective relationship with your boss and upper management, use the language of Business Results. Your boss is focused on performance and is expecting you to deliver it. Business results are primarily what your boss is evaluated on—what will deliver their success. You might not like this reality, but it is the nature of things. You need to convey how you will achieve these results in your communication with them. If you are not putting business results at the center of your conversations with your boss, you are likely not speaking the language that they understand and care about most.

Here are some recommended dos and don'ts for building a strong relationship with your boss.

Do	Don't
Set a clear strategic direction and align it with the organization's.	Provide lots of surprises.
Help others feel connected to the organization's purpose and future.	Overcommit and underdeliver.
Have the necessary skills and knowledge to perform job duties effectively.	Complain without offering a solution.
Be open to feedback and adjust behavior accordingly.	Underprepare for meetings.
Bring your best game each day.	Ignore your boss's pressures and aspirations.

Direct Reports

To build a relationship with your direct reports, use the language of People Results. Your employees care about the team dynamics, the level of engagement, career development, and how talent gets promoted on the team. Your team members want feedback and communication and to work in an environment that challenges and rewards. Yes, they also care about the performance outputs, but focusing on people results in your communication will get at the heart of what they care about; it will help you speak their language.

Here are some recommended dos and don'ts for building a strong relationship with your direct reports.

Do	Don't
Leverage the strengths of each team member.	Act like you are the smartest person in the room.
Treat others with dignity and respect.	Take all the credit but shift all the blame.
Create a working environment that motivates high performance.	Provide inconsistent or shifting priorities and expectations.
Be loyal to your people.	Tear down those on your team (in public or behind their back).
Remove obstacles and reduce their struggle in doing their jobs.	Feel like you must always make the decision.

Peers

To build a relationship with your peers, use the language of Internal Focus. Peers are concerned with how resources get allocated and how work gets accomplished internally. They want clarity on handoffs, transparency in budgeting, and your desire to partner to make things work better. Talking about team engagement may build some goodwill, but speaking about improving the day-to-day work patterns and fairly negotiating resources will get to the heart of what peers value most.

Here are some recommended dos and don'ts for building a strong relationship with your peers.

Do	Don't
Follow through on actions, promises, and assignments.	Compete against them to see who is better.
Accept responsibility for your actions and the actions of your team.	Try to be in charge and tell them what to do.
Communicate a compelling vision for partnering together.	Hoard resources and information.
Demonstrate high ethical standards.	Get frustrated and allow your emotions to go unfiltered.
Openly share knowledge and insights.	Avoid them to the detriment of your team.

Customers

To build a strong relationship with your customers, use the language of External Focus. This language concerns the broader marketplace in identifying the competitive landscape, industry trends, and current and future customer needs. Customers are less concerned about how something gets produced or if the team is happy. They want assurance that you know their concerns and hopes. They want to see action in satisfying their needs, even if it is a small amount. They also want to hear ideas on how you will address their desires in a cheaper, faster, or quicker manner.

Here are some recommended dos and don'ts for building a strong relationship with your customers.

Do	Don't
Align business goals to customer goals.	Hide behind a policy and not listen to their needs.
Be fair and open about issues and concerns.	Regard them as just another transaction instead of a longer relationship.
Know when to stop analyzing a problem and make a decision.	Ignore the competition or the alternatives they may have.
Apologize and identify possible solutions.	Assume you already know their wants and needs.
Live, lead, manage, and work with integrity.	Avoid answering hard questions.

An effective leader crafts messages based on those with whom they are speaking or working. The leader understands that the four different relationships each speak a different language and have unique needs. They know that using each relationship's unique language will improve understanding and lead to balanced performance. So, test it out. Adapt your communication approach based on the relationships you have and see the difference. They will appreciate how you speak their language!

The Leader as a Continual Learner

MANY PEOPLE are open to *learning*, but not all are interested in *developing*. You might ask, "Isn't learning the same thing as developing?" Not quite. There are really *two* levels to learning:

- The first level occurs when you hear, see, and/or experience something interesting or novel. It is often followed by the comment, "Wow, I didn't know that" or "That's cool."

- The second level of learning takes the new knowledge and *applies* it. Personal development is all about translating insight into action. It is the process of *doing* something with the information, transforming and integrating it into new or different behaviors, habits, and mindsets.

Not everyone readily jumps into the second level of learning and undertakes true personal development. It takes time, practice, and a lot of potential discomfort.

Learning from Lobsters

The metaphor of a lobster shedding its shell is a powerful way to depict this choice of real development.

As a young lobster grows, it becomes too large for the shell that protects it. The lobster must search for an area within the rocks on the floor of the ocean where it can feel relatively secure from any predators. Slowly, it begins to shed the shell, that which is stunting its growth.

Consider its plight when the shell is gone. Its new shell, which began growing before the old one was shed, is still soft and provides little protection. During this time, the lobster is extremely vulnerable and at great risk from predators. It is completely exposed to the dangerous world. Yet, the alternative would be worse. Without the periodic shedding of its shell, the lobster would not be able to grow and ultimately would perish.

As leaders, we are faced with a daily choice to grow. We are continually learning new information and deciding if and how we do something with it. How can development be structured to create a safe environment for a leader to shed their shell and grow?

To help leaders make this important choice and feel that being vulnerable is worth it, we have identified six secrets for achieving lasting personal development. These principles can foster the right environment, attitude, and actions to achieve Level 2 learning. These also become the foundation for lasting individual *and* company-wide training and development solutions.

Six Secrets to Personal Growth

1: Everyday Practice

Development is far more than a single event or training class. It is an everyday effort to practice, practice, practice. Consistently spending time on a skill or new way of thinking is key. For example, learning to ask open-ended questions to foster more open dialogue on your team is not a thing you can just decide to do, like snapping your fingers; it is a new habit in which it can take weeks to achieve proficiency.

2: Alignment with Team and Organization

Get in sync with your team, boss, and organization so your development can be supported and sustained. How many of us come back from a conference with a long list of great ideas and the next day they all go out the window? It is critical to gain feedback and insight from others in the organization and to find out what they value. They can advocate for you instead of against you. And aligning with the current power structure will best position you to appropriately push back, developing yourself and others simultaneously.

3: Motivation

Development should happen because *you* want it, not because someone told you it's necessary. Mandatory development rarely works. If you don't have an internal desire for personal development, you may go through the motions, but you won't receive much benefit. Reach deep inside and find or create the motivation to learn and apply good ideas to help you be a better leader.

4: Positivity

Engaging in development can and should be seen as a positive experience that will lead to a better way of working. Spending time on development is an investment in the future. Having the right attitude about development will help you reap the greatest value from it.

5: Tailored Individual Development

Each person brings myriad unique experiences, successes, and concerns. Crafting development experiences to fit the needs of each person builds on their strengths and addresses their specific areas for opportunities. The more tailored the development, the greater level of respect and value the leader will feel.

6: Discomfort

When speaking to groups, we sometimes tell them that we hope they feel uncomfortable today, because that is a strong sign that development is occurring! Lasting personal development pushes you beyond your comfort zone. It stretches and expands your capabilities and is strong evidence that learning has transitioned into behavior-changing development.

The Five Steps of Personal Change

Over the years, we have witnessed countless attempts by professionals from all walks of life to change some aspect of their behavior in leading others. Studying why some have failed while others have succeeded reveals tremendously helpful insights. We realized there are five steps that are essential for sustained personal change in any aspect of life.

Following all five of these steps will help anyone making lasting personal behavior change. All five are essential—especially the last one.

Step 1: Awareness. You have to be aware that there is a problem or concern. It is like putting on your pants and noticing that they are too tight. Perhaps you have gained a few pounds.

Step 2: Desire. You must desire to do something about the problem because you are dissatisfied with the current status. This desire can originate either externally (pressures from your organization or boss) or internally (personal goals or interests—for example, you want to look and feel healthier).

Step 3: Skills & Resources. Once you are aware of a problem and want to change, you need to get the resources and skills to prepare you for action. Continuing the weight gain example, you would want to understand calories and diet as well as get a gym membership or understand what kinds of exercise you can do.

Step 4: Action. Now that you are armed with awareness, desire, and new resources and skills, you put these tools to work by setting reasonable, encouraging goals. Start making small changes. You could start to work out four times a week and also stop eating dessert. Unfortunately, this is the step where people often fizzle out. They make it this far but can't stick with it. They become discouraged; they let old habits take over, the needs of the day soon dominate, and little is changed. *The key to sustained personal change is in the final step.*

Step 5: Support. No matter how strong-minded you are, there will come a point at which you need the encouragement of others to help you continue. Sharing your goal or commitment with a trusted friend, asking them to keep you on track, is the final piece of the formula for personal success. In those moments of weakness or discouragement, your supportive associate will kindly yet firmly watch out for you, encourage you, and provide the support over time that you seek (especially to help you keep on with your healthy behaviors!). If you ignore this final step, the sustained pursuit of your goal will die over time. For you to accomplish the change you desire, this final step makes all the difference in the world. But support is not just an individual-to-individual activity. Personal or group support is just one kind. There is also organizational or structural support: the support from policies, procedures, and rules of the organization you work for, or the structure of your habits and friends. Design your life so that it's easier to do what will help you reach your goal than to not do it.

Tips to Help You on Your Journey

As you read through this book, think about your own development and create an action plan with these learning tips in mind:

1 Select something you have a desire to change or develop. Without a desire to change, you will likely not stick with it.

2 Only work on one or two areas at a time. Having too many priorities often means no priorities.

3 Identify one to three measurable activities for each area. Goals without performance measures rarely succeed.

4 Leverage your strengths and minimize the impact of your weaknesses. Most professionals succeed by using their strengths. Excessive focus on weaknesses erodes and dilutes your powerful strengths.

5 Be very specific and concrete about areas you wish to improve or focus on. Specific, concrete details will keep you focused on your goals.

6 Start with small changes and progress to larger changes. As Desmond Tutu said, there is only one way to eat an elephant: a bite at a time.

7 Identify roadblocks that may prevent the development plan from happening. Every path to success has potholes, speed bumps, and roadblocks; anticipate and prepare for them if you want to reach your goal.

8 Consider creating ways to work around your weaknesses by utilizing others' strengths—building your team to offset your shortcomings or delegating tasks to others with strengths you don't have. A key function of a team is to mold strengths and weaknesses of all members so that, collectively, the team achieves true synergy.

9 Select people to follow up with you—a mentor, boss, consultant, coach, peer, or friend. Your motivation and willpower will fluctuate; working with a partner will strengthen both.

10 Tell others what your development plan is—the more you share your plan, the greater the chance it will happen. Establishing external expectations and accountability will help you stay committed in moments of vacillation.

11 Learn from watching or reading about others who excel in the areas you wish to develop. You can avoid pitfalls and gain valuable insights by learning from others who have mastered the areas you are working on.

12 Remember you can't be amazing at everything. You are human; give yourself a break.

13 Celebrate successes along the way. Small celebrations recharge your commitment.

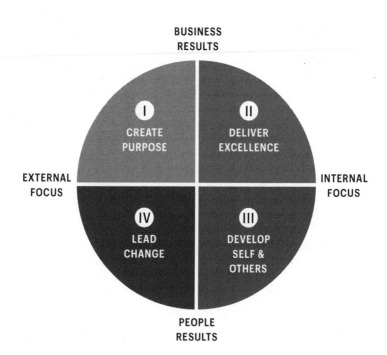

PART II

THE
21 DIMENSIONS

Each of the following chapters is dedicated
to one of the 21 Leadership Dimensions.
Each chapter is organized into the following sections:

An overview of the Dimension

What it is

What it is not

How it looks when it is overused

Coaching Tips

Self-assessment

Action-planning notes

QUADRANT I
CREATE PURPOSE

---

1   Customer Focus
2   Effective Communication
3   Presentation Skills
4   Strategic Thinking

Dimension 1
Customer Focus

"Take care of your customer
or somebody else will."

ANONYMOUS

How well do I know my customers?
Who are my internal customers?
How much time do I spend focusing on my customers?

What Is Customer Focus?

Customer focus is constant awareness of customer needs and cultivation of customer relationships. It's knowing that your internal and external customers are the lifeblood of your business and must be central in all strategic organizational decisions. These relationships must be researched, understood, and nurtured. This gives you the ability to deliver your product or service in such a way that you fulfill the needs, wants, and values of your customer better than anyone else.

What it looks like:

- Aligning organizational vision and goals with current and future customer needs

- Identifying how competitors are addressing your customers' needs

- Knowing and partnering with your customers to create the best solutions

- Informing your customers of problems and proposed solutions in a timely manner

What it is not:

- Viewing your customer as only a sale

- Covering up the truth when things go wrong

- Relying more on a hunch than on research

- Assuming they will continue with you because of your shared history

What it looks like when it is overused:

- Rapidly adjusting to meet customer demands at the expense of agreed strategy

- Blaming fellow employees in front of customers to show you are on the customer's side

- Consistently overpromising and underdelivering

- Providing the same time and attention to each customer no matter their size or impact on your organization

When you focus on your customers, you can drive better business and people performance. Here are some of the results you can achieve.

Business results:

- Initial, repeat, and aftermarket sales
- Customer satisfaction
- Customer loyalty and retention
- Mutual confidence and trust

People results:

- Long-term internal and external partnerships
- Cross-functional collaboration
- Employee engagement and productivity
- Innovative thinking

Coaching Tips

Knowing Your Customer and Building the Relationship

1 Proactively partner with your customers in resolving problems.

2 Always ... always ... always listen to your customers.

3 Don't assume you already know what your customer wants and needs.

4 Frequently solicit formal and informal feedback from your customers on what they truly want, how they want it, and how you're doing.

5 Look for marketplace cues and signals to assess and prepare for changing attitudes and preferences by your customers.

6 Anticipate and proactively address your customers' needs and concerns—including the ones they have not thought of.

7 Meet frequently to clarify, assess, and improve your performance and deliverables.

8 Level with your customers when mistakes are made. They will likely work with you. If you're not honest and straight with them, however, their trust in you can be severely damaged. It all comes down to trust!

9 Be mindful of your attitude—you can't hide it. Your customers will judge you on your attitude toward them, yourself, and your team and organization.

10 Always do what you say you will do.

11 Go the extra mile. This is especially true with tough customers. Win them over.

12 Put yourself in the shoes of your customer. What would you like to know and be made aware of, and when? How would you prefer to receive news?

Maintaining and Building Your Customer Base

13 Plan your business around the needs of your current and future customers.

14 Be aware of every area of your organization—including its culture—that can or should be adapted to anticipate and meet evolving customer needs brought about by global, national, and local economic change, emerging technologies, and industry trends.

15 Align your quality assurance to meet demands of current and prospective customers.

16 Focus policies and processes on exceeding customer expectations.

17 Establish methods and behaviors to provide a satisfying customer experience at every touchpoint—so your customer will want more.

18 Measure customer satisfaction through reliable and tested metrics.

19 Avoid trying to wow customers with a dazzling array of complexity. Sell them on the simple concepts they want to buy.

20 Decide what you can and cannot deliver and be consistent and reliable in doing it.

21 Establish key points of contact among your customers. Rely on them for information, opinions, perceptions, suggestions, and general feedback. Use them as sounding boards to try out new ideas. Ask their opinions on challenges you face.

22 Treat customer complaints as a gift. What can you learn from them?

23 Train and empower your team to promptly resolve or escalate customer problems, concerns, or frustrations.

24 Proactively and quickly inform customers of schedule changes, problems, or setbacks. Failing to keep them up-to-date can promote distrust and suspicion.

25 To make sure customers are completely satisfied, *follow up*!

Being More Competitive

26 Look at and learn from your competition. Analyze where they are in the marketplace, and why. What are they doing well and where are they slipping?

27 Learn the techniques your competition is using to gather accurate data on customer service.

28 Periodically meet with your team and other business groups to analyze your customers, markets, and competitive trends. Assess how your customer base may shift.

29 Initiate a session with your team to discuss and analyze what would be needed upon entering new markets. This will help you prepare for potential opportunities.

30 Seek feedback from former customers on how to better deliver, especially from ones you've just lost.

31 Create and follow through on aftermarketing strategies.

Focusing on Your Internal Customer and Culture

32 Optimize external customer satisfaction by first cultivating your internal customer relationships and a customer focused, service-oriented organization culture.

33 Treat your own people as you want them to treat external customers and other internal customers. This will promote an engaged, productive, customer-focused workforce.

34 Examine your culture. How are you, your group, and your company regarded by others with respect to integrity, fair practices, innovation, and service?

35 Ask yourself: Will your organization's culture attract new customers and new talent?

36 Establish metrics/processes for employee feedback on your organization's culture—a powerful force that can work for or against you.

 ## Self-Assessment

Using the scale provided, rate yourself on the following leadership behaviors.

POOR   EXCELLENT

1   2   3   4   5   6   7

____ I am focused on the needs of the customer.
____ I know the needs of each of my customer groups.
____ I plan my business based on my customers' needs.
____ I review my business based on my customers' needs.
____ I analyze information about my customers.
____ I gather feedback from my customers.

Comments

_____
_____
_____
_____
_____
_____
_____
_____
_____
_____
_____
_____
_____
_____
_____

Action-Planning Notes

Which three things in this section will help you be a better leader?

1

_____

_____

_____

2

_____

_____

_____

3

_____

_____

_____

What would change if you started or continued doing these three things?

_____

_____

_____

_____

How can you implement these changes?

_____

_____

_____

Dimension 2
Effective Communication

"The biggest hurdle to effective communication
is the assumption that it has taken place."

ANONYMOUS

Do I have a consistent plan for clear, concise, timely communications?

Do I seek clarification on how the messages are received?

Do I consider the needs and feelings of others when communicating?

What Is Effective Communication?

It is the ability to clearly express targeted messages, at the right time, using the right media, and the right venues. It requires follow-through and feedback to ensure understanding and stakeholder alignment. It's recognizing that every aspect of your business relies on the effective exchange of information. Your communication skills in all your workplace relationships are crucial to your overall success as a leader.

What it looks like:

- Communicating clearly and concisely

- Using the most relevant medium for your audience

- Seeking clarification on how the message was received

- Balancing phone and electronic communication with face-to-face time

What it is not:

- Minimizing communication planning

- Overusing the same approach despite ineffective results

- Ignoring nonverbal cues

- Assuming others think, understand, and respond the ways you do

What it looks like when it is overused:

- Repeating the same words without checking for understanding

- Sending more emails and having more meetings that don't change the results

- Including too much detail and obscuring the main point under the banner of transparency

- Attempting to not offend or upset anyone at all

When you communicate effectively, you can drive better business and people performance. Here are some of the results you can achieve.

Business results:

- Clear direction and goals
- Aligned business units
- Improved productivity and effectiveness
- Customer satisfaction

People results:

- Informed teams
- Active and timely feedback
- Spirit of collaboration
- Improved internal and external relationships

Coaching Tips

Strategies and Tactics for Effective Communication

1 Give whomever you're speaking with 100 percent of your attention—be present. They will watch, far more than you realize, to see if you listen to them.

2 Recognize that they may not always remember what you say, but they'll remember how you made them feel. This is often a result of your tone, demeanor, and demonstration of respect for their needs and input.

3 Have a tested, reliable plan to provide communication of all vital information to key internal and external stakeholders. Keep the frequency and media up-to-date.

4 Create communication guidelines and messaging that reflect—and are respectful of—intergenerational communication styles and modes and evolving diversity issues.

5 Be alert to leading-edge social media and electronic communication tools, and adjust your plan and messages accordingly.

6 Design messages that clearly convey your vision, direction, priorities, and objectives—combined with how you're creating value for your audience.

7 Consider people's unique backgrounds, perspectives, functions, styles, successes, disappointments, and feelings. Tailor your messages accordingly.

8 Be ready to summarize your purpose or request in one to two sentences.

9 Ask yourself: What will produce the best result—a *presentation* or a *conversation*? They are distinctly different and will produce different results.

10 Be inclusive of remote employees, contract employees, and volunteers. They have unique needs for feeling included and valued.

11 As you deliver your message or directive, regularly check for possible confusion as well as reluctance or fear in expressing opposing views.

12 Make your messages more believable and genuine with nonverbal cues that match your words, and tune in to nonverbal messages from your audience.

13 Appoint a "recorder" in your meetings to keep track of action items.

14 Adapt your interpersonal style to best fit the style of others—your bosses, direct reports, peers, customers, and other associates.

15 Suspend judgment as you listen to others and reluctantly interrupt or talk over them.

16 Use silence as a powerful conversation tool. Know when to speak, when to listen, and when to be silent, to improve your ability to lead others to higher levels of performance. Silence allows them to respond.

Communicating as a Leader

17 Share your clear vision, direction, and priorities for your organization, and confirm that your team understands. Giving them the "why" will increase their understanding.

18 Overcommunicate your organization's mission and live it consistently through your messaging and actions.

19 Recognize that as a leader, everything you say is "on the record"—at a restaurant, at a bar, in the office, on a business trip, or at a social gathering. Use care and restraint.

20 "Walk the talk." Make sure your actions and values match what you say. People watch you and formulate opinions of your leadership based on your consistency.

21 Foster an effective team by creating a climate of open information exchange—with each other, across departments, and across the organization.

22 Share information with your team that indirectly affects them—for example, facts about other groups or customers with whom they interact.

23 Plan "Management by Walking Around" (MBWA) times into your schedule. Have informal chats to exchange information, feel the pulse of the organization, listen to opinions, and learn of concerns.

24 Ask your employees to tell you what they need to complete tasks and assignments. Be open and responsive to their inputs and questions. Don't let them feel it is a bother to you or they may stop communicating with you.

25 Follow up and follow through with your people and with all stakeholders on communications that are important to them.

26 Share the essence of your key messages when day-to-day opportunities arise for appropriate, informal internal and external conversations.

27 Ask your boss, colleagues, and customers how they prefer to be kept informed—how often, how much detail, by what method, and by whom.

28 Have a frank discussion to learn your boss's definition of "urgent." Clarify their priorities and respond accordingly.

29 Never shoot the messenger. Reinforce them for their honesty and forthrightness. This will ensure that you are not kept out of the loop in the future.

Avoiding Roadblocks to Effective Communication

30 Recognize that the biggest hurdle to effective communication is the assumption that it has taken place. Test your assumptions about your communication efforts.

31 Put down your mobile device during your conversations. Give your full attention.

32 Be aware of messages you send nonverbally that can conflict with the intent of your communication. It's possible to give unintended signals.

33 Attack the problem, not the person's style, communication techniques, or delivery.

34 Analyze communication breakdowns. Why have they occurred? How can they be prevented in the future? Involve others in your analysis as part of the solution.

35 Make sure your meetings are not one-way data-dumping sessions. Meetings should involve discussion. Otherwise, save everyone's time by using email.

36 Don't allow one individual to dominate a discussion. Politely thank the person for their thoughts and invite others to express their views.

37 Recognize when you are angry; do *not* speak or take action until your anger is under control. This will save you regrettable moments.

38 Keep in mind that others hear what you're saying with their own preconceived notions and differing perspectives that may distort your intended meaning. Seek clarification periodically.

39 Embrace the efficiency of electronic messaging but avoid using it when face-to-face or phone interactions are more appropriate. Encourage your team to do the same.

40 Don't put off bad news or neglect to keep people informed when there's no news. No one likes surprises: people would rather get timely bad news than no news and be caught off-guard later.

41 Don't assume that the same message delivered the same way will always be successful for every audience.

Self-Assessment

Using the scale provided, rate yourself on the following leadership behaviors.

POOR   EXCELLENT

1   2   3   4   5   6   7

____ I listen for understanding before I respond.

____ I keep stakeholders up-to-date.

____ I balance my use of email, texting, instant messaging, face-to-face, and phone communications.

____ I ask open-ended questions and allow space for others to respond.

____ I am concise and clear in my communication.

____ I stay on message when addressing a group.

Comments

_____

_____

_____

_____

_____

_____

_____

_____

_____

Action-Planning Notes

What three things in this section will help you be a better leader?

1

_____

_____

_____

2

_____

_____

_____

3

_____

_____

_____

What would change if you started or continued doing these three things?

_____

_____

_____

_____

How can you implement these changes?

_____

_____

_____

_____

Dimension 3
Presentation Skills

"Regardless of the changes in technology, the market
for well-crafted messages will always have an audience."

STEVE BURNETT

How well do I know and connect with my audience?
Am I clear about my desired outcomes?
Do I anticipate and prepare for questions?

What Are Presentation Skills?

A vital part of being a great leader is the ability to communicate prepared or impromptu messages that connect with large or small audiences to drive desired outcomes. Building an informative, persuasive presentation requires clear focus on your goal combined with careful analysis of your audience to tailor an approach that will appeal to their point of view.

Presenting in front of a group lets others know you, your ideas, the strength of your personality, and your potential for greater responsibility.

What it looks like:

- Organizing your information for smooth flow and delivery
- Maintaining a clear and relevant message throughout the presentation
- Engaging the audience with appropriate interaction
- Answering questions in a concise way

What it is not:

- Generalizing the message without specific information
- Disregarding the audience and their expectations
- Ignoring data to support claims or recommendations
- Being unprepared to address concerns or different opinions

What it looks like when it is overused:

- Preparing so much that you sound scripted or inflexible
- Showing impatience with or apathy toward your own presentation
- Focusing too much on just one person or faction of the audience
- Sharing more examples than needed to convey the point

With excellent presentation skills, you can drive better business and people performance. Here are some of the results you can achieve.

Business results:

- Selling ideas to key decision makers
- Winning and retaining customers
- Using data and stories to persuade others
- Strengthening your career potential

People results:

- Uniting others around a common purpose
- Inspiring engagement in a change effort
- Motivating performance excellence
- Building a strong executive presence and influence

Coaching Tips

Building an Effective Presentation

1 Ask yourself what will generate the best result—a *presentation* or a *conversation*?

2 Reflect on prior presentations you've made—with both pleasant and unpleasant outcomes. What contributed to each type? Can you apply it now? Which lessons do you not want to forget or overlook?

3 Identify what you want your audience to take away from your presentation.

4 Develop a grabber to open your presentation. Choose attention-getting techniques—photos, stories, metaphors, dramatic examples, comparisons, statistics, or personal experiences—that will most appeal to your audience.

5 Plan to begin your presentation by 1) expressing your appreciation for something specific that your audience has recently done, and 2) establishing something in common

with your audience by sharing a mutual experience or outlook with them.

6 Summarize your real purpose in one sentence; state it at the beginning and repeat it at the conclusion.

7 As you prepare your content, group your ideas into natural categories, with headings, to ensure the logical flow of information. Make sure each heading supports your overarching purpose.

8 Use compelling evidence (that has been double-checked) as you build your case.

9 Keep in mind that every person is unique. Consider and address their individual needs, including intergenerational and diversity factors, when crafting your message.

10 Identify biases and specific attitudes of your audience to anticipate their concerns, hot buttons, and emotional issues.

11 Anticipate your audience's questions and weave the answers into your content.

12 Ask colleagues to hear your rehearsals. Have them ask you questions that come to mind and share their thoughts on weak and strong points.

13 Ask yourself and your colleagues what the average person will likely remember thirty minutes after hearing your presentation. They might not remember much of what you say, but they'll always remember how you made them feel.

Earning Audience Engagement

14 Make sure your audience can answer: "Is there anything new here?" "What's in it for me, my team, and the company?"

15 Establish credibility with how you are introduced and your vocal authority, tone, manner, and conviction.

16 Adjust your tone, pace, and style to the audience.

17 Let your audience feel your energy and enthusiasm. They'll usually remember that long after your words are forgotten.

18 Learn if your audience prefers numbers or words, statistics or stories, no nonsense or a touch of emotion.

19 Resist giving the same speech to differing audiences. Study each audience's makeup, background, level of sophistication, education, concerns, friendliness, and emotions.

20 Be likable—that's the number one element people look for.

Presenting with Polish

21 Become aware of annoying or distracting habits or speech patterns in your delivery or style. Learn this from trusted colleagues or seeing yourself on video. Recognizing these tendencies is the first powerful step to overcoming them.

22 Keep it brief. It's better to go under the allotted time than over it.

23 PowerPoint presentations can be effective if designed stylishly and used properly with an emphasis on imagery.

24 Before the presentation, become familiar with the room you'll be in: size, shape, external noise, windows, sunlight, podium, tables, lighting, riser to stand on, AV and other equipment, furniture arrangement, microphone, and climate controls.

25 Ensure that the room is prepared with equipment, props, and resources you and your audience will need.

26 Practice! Privately rehearse your delivery out loud. Reading it to yourself silently doesn't allow your mouth and tongue to become familiar with the phrases you need to emphasize. Where feasible, record your rehearsals.

27 Avoid giving the appearance that you're reading the material.

28 Remain cool when challenged and when controversial topics arise. Never be defensive.

29 Manage your nerves (breathe deeply, drink water, use finger and hand exercises).

30 Be aware that the physiological responses to nervousness and stress are identical. Your body is gearing up properly for the presentation. Your natural, expected nervous energy brings animation to your presentation. Fretting over it will only increase it.

Communicating the Message Effectively

31 As a rule for complete communication, follow the five "Ws" of journalism: who, what, when, where, and why. Be aware that people have an innate need to understand and internalize the "why" behind your purpose or proposal.

32 Speak on subjects you know. Otherwise it may be apparent and will damage your credibility and reputation.

33 Communicate using the language of the people you're addressing.

34 Jokes and humor should be used carefully and sparingly. Humor often backfires and is misunderstood—which can make you look foolish.

35 Tell them what you are going to say, say it, and tell them what you have said.

36 Prepare for unforeseen reactions by some of your audience. In a hostile or negative situation, maintain personal control and respond with respect and professionalism.

37 During a question-and-answer period, answer honestly and directly. If you don't know the answer, admit it and commit to finding out and replying soon.

38 When answering a question, say what you do know or what needs to be considered to help identify the solution—you don't always have to have the right answer.

Concluding a Presentation

39 Summarize by restating your core purpose and telling them what you have said.

40 In a presentation where assignments are made, as the leader, ensure everyone is on track by asking questions. Take the time to clarify that there is understanding.

41 Include a clear call to action.

42 Use a strong closing sentence to create a lasting impression.

43 Avoid asking: "Are there any questions?" Instead ask a more specific question like: "How can this benefit you?" or "What is one way this could impact your team?"

44 Seek feedback after your presentation on how you handled your content, your delivery, key points, examples, technology, maintaining focus, time constraints, questions, objections, and other audience reactions.

45 Use feedback on your performance and seek other opportunities to learn and grow in delivering strong presentations that will advance your credibility and your career.

Self-Assessment

Using the scale provided, rate yourself on the following leadership behaviors.

POOR   EXCELLENT

1   2   3   4   5   6   7

____ I adjust my presentations based on the audience.
____ I am clear about my main message.
____ I am clear about my desired outcomes.
____ I use metaphors or stories to illustrate major points.
____ I practice, practice, practice.
____ I avoid reading the material.
____ I am prepared and confident when responding to questions.
____ I ask for feedback and welcome it.

Comments

_____

_____

_____

_____

_____

_____

_____

_____

_____

_____

_____

_____

_____

_____

Action-Planning Notes

What three things in this section will help you be a better leader?

1

_____

_____

_____

2

_____

_____

_____

3

_____

_____

_____

What would change if you started or continued doing these three things?

_____

_____

_____

_____

How can you implement these changes?

_____

_____

_____

_____

Dimension 4
Strategic Thinking

"The best way to predict
the future is to create it."

PETER DRUCKER

Do I frequently review directions and objectives to
continually add value?

Do I question the status quo?

Do I stay on top of the competitive landscape?

What Is Strategic Thinking?

Strategic thinking is connecting abstract ideas to create
actionable patterns that drive future business. It requires the
wisdom and ability to devise and balance short- and long-term
plans. It is based in organizational, competitive, and socioeconomic analysis. It's asking insightful questions, anticipating

and planning for change, and focusing team energy to maximize your organization's ongoing position in the marketplace. It's thinking like a CEO.

What it looks like:

* Anticipating how to add value continually for customers and stakeholders

* Questioning if the current solution is still the best. Balancing new ideas with self-confidence and openness to feedback

* Setting short- and long-term goals with tactics to fulfill your strategies

* Seeking to create a world-class organization

What it is not:

* Focusing only on reacting to day-to-day responsibilities

* Neglecting long-term planning or follow-through

* Ignoring or discounting market trends and demographic value changes

* Following impulsive decisions without questioning validity

What it looks like when it is overused:

* Changing strategic direction on a weekly, monthly, or quarterly basis

* Spending six to twelve months developing a beautiful strategic plan

* Involving everyone in the strategic planning process

* Minimizing or neglecting cash flow in favor of longer-term thinking

When you think strategically, you can drive better business and people performance. Here are some of the results you can achieve.

Business results:

- Anticipating and meeting customers' needs
- Identifying root issues
- Defining and optimizing strategic goals
- Managing risk

People results:

- Promoting new and different thinking
- Engaging and retaining employees
- Aligning accountability and follow-through on assignments
- Leading teams to tackle issues proactively

Coaching Tips

Thinking Strategically

1 Look at your organization from the perspective of your most loyal customers—the focal point of your business. What understanding does this new vantage point give you?

2 When making a decision that affects your organization, consider both short-term effects and long-term ramifications.

3 Challenge the status quo and support measured risks.

4 Identify what you will stop or not do at all. That is the essence of good strategy. Assess your personal risk tendencies in the range of "risk avoidance" to "risk seeking."

5 Avoid looking for a quick fix to address problems. Instead, look at the broader context in considering options and new directions. Be open to nontraditional solutions.

6 Get a greater sense of your organization by looking at it from a 500-foot perspective and then a 50,000-foot perspective. Notice that the higher you go, the broader your view becomes—you're removing yourself from your daily challenges and appreciating the entire operation, moving from "tactical" to "strategic" in your thinking.

7 Get big-picture perspective, but don't lose sight of important details that support the overarching purpose of your organization.

8 Involve your group. Solicit ideas and views from them in developing strategies for:

- customer focus
- risk
- group direction
- change
- group support

9 Consider and apply these four essential strategic thinking skills in reviewing possible solutions:

- intuitive thinking
- conceptual thinking
- critical thinking
- creative thinking

10 Shift your perspective from day-to-day firefighting to long-term planning.

11 Consider the following factors:

- customer needs and demands
- workforce and organization culture
- competitors
- technology (current and future)

- global and local socioeconomics
- logistics
- suppliers/business partners
- offshoring/onshoring
- resources
- regulations

12 Discuss business strategies with your boss or other senior managers to develop a feel for the organization's short- and long-term status and future.

13 Discuss some of your challenges with those who are formally working in strategic endeavors or initiatives in your organization. Solicit their ideas. Have them teach you their views and methods.

Short-Term Strategic Thinking

14 Stay current via business journals, newspapers, blogs, podcasts, and media reports; follow futurists; study market trends. Analyze the data and be proactive to grow the business.

15 Track and analyze customer satisfaction.

16 Analyze how all the functional groups in your organization affect each other. What purposes and coordinated efforts do they have beyond the obvious? Where are the handoff points and most essential linkages? How can you improve synergy?

17 Identify your team's prevailing paradigms and attitudes. Decide if any are antiquated or obsolete, and replace, redefine, or reinforce.

18 Be aware of the financial condition and general budget issues of the organization.

19 Know your own department's financial performance and its impact on the organization.

20 Consider the views of customers and stakeholders.

21 Analyze processes, systems, behaviors, patterns, technology, and communication flow to diagnose weakness and improvement opportunities. Which should be implemented across the enterprise?

22 Break problems apart into smaller pieces; find the root cause and you've found your real problem.

23 Identify critical success factors for your group, with measures and targets for each initiative and program. Select and align your team accordingly.

24 Question traditional methods and seek global best practices.

25 Analyze your value chain processes for ways to improve efficiencies and your end product or service.

26 Meet with your suppliers and other business partners to assess the value chain flow and identify mutually profitable actions.

Long-Term Strategic Thinking

27 Look at opportunities and issues from a broad perspective. Anticipate and plan for possible reactions to them from the marketplace, analysts, industry observers, outsiders, insiders, associates, and stakeholders.

28 Design a detailed analysis of your major competitors. Examine comparative metrics. What are their competitive advantages? Where does your company excel? Where does it need strengthening?

29 Identify key market trends, opportunities, and organizational capabilities that collectively would bring significant competitive advantage to the organization.

30 Develop a global perspective to your business even though you may not be directly involved to that degree. Consider cross-cultural implications and attitudes to prepare you for the future, avoid limited vision, and expand your ideas and thinking. How do people (customers and employees) think from cultures outside of your comfort zone?

31 Identify the critical components of what you define as your successful organizational strategy. Determine how each component is performing, and adding value to the organization's goals and objectives. Identify where each is struggling or vulnerable.

32 Expand your thinking and perspective to go far beyond grasping your own competitors. Think deeply about the entire industry. Analyze the entire complex of like businesses, as everyone is linked with each other. Go beyond what you and your team normally do. Reach the next level of complexity. See what you discover and apply it to your current and future direction.

33 Periodically look at the ability of your suppliers/business partners to meet projected requirements. Probe deeply to ensure assumptions won't lead to disappointment or failure as you grow. Test it. Be certain. Your future success depends on it.

34 Explore with your team any limitations you've imposed on your organization's progress and success. Are they accepted ruts that your predecessors placed years ago and that need to be removed?

35 Have your employees share their competitive organization and business strategies with you and your team to assess their strategic orientation. Understand their innovative thinking and see if it is aligned with the rest of the enterprise.

36 Ensure that your team supports and understands the plan so they can clearly articulate it to their teams. Welcome ideas, inputs, criticisms, and suggestions from employees on improving your organization's strategies and ideas. Don't rely on the old suggestion box. Have skip-level meetings and brown-bag lunches with various groups of employees to seek and encourage their ideas.

Avoiding Obstacles to Strategic Thinking

37 Once you've weighed and accepted the risks, avoid second-guessing a decision or action and becoming preoccupied with the possible negative outcomes.

38 Don't limit the exposure of your strategic ideas to a selected few. Communicate them to your workforce so they feel involved and can add their implementation ideas.

39 Don't limit your thinking to competing with your competitors or gaining market share. Take your thinking to a new level of creating novel opportunities. Creating will open you to entirely new horizons over merely competing.

40 Start with trusting and leveraging your organization's core competencies as the foundation of your strategic vision and focus.

41 Don't be reluctant to make the tough calls and choices.

Self-Assessment

Using the scale provided, rate yourself on the following leadership behaviors.

POOR   EXCELLENT

1   2   3   4   5   6   7

____ I regularly scan outside market forces and the competitive landscape.

____ I regularly assess the current and future needs of our customers/stakeholders.

____ I align initiatives to the needs of our customers/stakeholders.

____ I regularly review and update our strategic direction and objectives.

____ I use a scorecard to measure the success of business and people performance.

Comments

_____

_____

_____

_____

_____

_____

_____

_____

Action-Planning Notes

What three things in this section will help you be a better leader?

1
_____
_____
_____

2
_____
_____
_____

3
_____
_____
_____

What would change if you started or continued doing these three things?

_____
_____
_____
_____

How can you implement these changes?

_____
_____
_____
_____

QUADRANT II
DELIVER EXCELLENCE

Dimension 5
Decision Making

Do I know when to stop analyzing and make a decision?

Am I willing to take a stand on critical issues?

Do I know when to delegate or take a team approach to
decision making?

What Is Decision Making?

Decision making is the ability to understand why a decision
needs to be made as well as how to define, analyze, implement, and communicate the decision to those affected by its
outcomes. It requires balancing information with intuition and

knowing when to stop analyzing a problem and make a decision. Your decisions can affect more than the present issue and you need to consider what those effects might be. The impact and buy-in of your decisions will determine their effectiveness.

What it looks like:

* Gauging involvement based on who will be impacted

* Determining when a decision is ready to be implemented

* Maintaining focus while balancing time requirements and/ or incomplete data

* Achieving consensus through open dialogue

What it is not:

* Delaying or not making a decision at all
* Relying solely on opinion or tradition
* Allowing debate and discussion without an end
* Saying you agree with a decision that you expect to fail

How it looks when it is overused:

* Ensuring everyone's voice is heard before making all decisions

* Making rapid decisions for complex problems in the name of decisiveness

* Thinking "I'm smart and therefore what I decide will be right"

* Trusting only one source of information for all decisions

Through effective decision making, you can drive better business and people performance. Here are some of the results you can achieve.

Business results:

* Prioritizing short- and long-term goals

* Delivering strategies and plans for improved business performance

* Establishing accountability

* Driving productivity and change

People results:

* Achieving alignment through effective communication
* Gauging and securing commitment from others
* Leveraging the strengths and expertise of the team
* Staff engagement, empowerment, and development

Coaching Tips

Pre-Decision Analysis

1 Recognize the difference between expensive and less costly decisions. Give ample time to decisions that are expensive to make. Make less costly decisions quickly, at the lowest level possible; delegate.

2 Involve those whom the decision will affect in the decision-making process. People tend to support what they help create.

3 Make sure your decision and its outcome are consistent with your organization's values and code of ethics.

4 Determine who could kill your decision before you tackle it.

5 Create a brainstorming atmosphere in which no idea is eliminated or critiqued in the early stages, especially by the leader.

6 Invite fresh, innovative perspectives from people from varied levels and backgrounds.

7 Sleep on a difficult decision to make sure it is your best choice. Let your brain work on it as you sleep.

8 Check your intuition and common sense.

9 Consider combining the most desirable aspects of two or more alternatives.

10 Anticipate when a decision may be controversial. Treat it as a consultative decision, and do not make it without gathering enough data from all sides to allow for a fair and thorough analysis.

11 Seek reactions and opinions from trusted colleagues prior to implementing critical decisions. Give them permission to provide completely candid feedback.

12 Mentally rehearse how the decision will play out if enacted. Visualize all possible consequences. Consider this a dress rehearsal and test of the implementation.

13 Know when to stop analyzing an issue, make the decision, act on it, and own it.

Implementing a Decision

14 Recognizing implementation as a vital aspect of decision making, coordinate:

- an announcement to those affected
- commitment of those involved
- resources needed
- schedule and timing

15 Have a well-thought-out plan for your response to antici-
pated resistance.

16 Create a process to track your decisions and their outcomes.
Look for trends and analyze your general decision-making
style.

17 Strive for consensus among your team, but when indeci-
siveness prevails, make the call and expect your team to
support the decision.

18 If you feel scared or anxious about the decision, write down
your fears and worries and categorize them. How legit-
imate are they? Recognize how your emotions can cloud
the process, hinder the analysis, dilute the data, and distort
the final outcome.

19 Look for people who tend to be rebels or mavericks. Invite
their opinions. Consider how they think. What drives their
views? Respect their contrary attitudes. They will stretch
you and help you see totally different perspectives.

20 Become skeptical of those who always agree with you. They
do not stretch you or your thinking, or add fresh ideas.

21 Ask yourself how often you backpedal on decisions. Are you
seeing a trend?

22 Own decisions you are involved with even if you don't agree
with the final decision.

23 Don't ask others for their input or ideas if you have already
decided the end result. They may feel used or patronized if
they discover that you were not sincere in involving them.

24 View "no decision" as a decision. It is an option and carries
a message.

Fostering a Decisive Team

25 Encourage healthy dissent, but once the debate ends, ensure everyone walks out of the meeting with wholehearted commitment to the decision.

26 Use a team approach to decision making when:

- you lack adequate information
- the decision will directly affect the whole team
- you need creative input
- time allows the team to confer
- you will need the team's support in the final decision and its implementation

27 Don't use a team approach when:

- the decision is routine
- time does not allow for it
- you honestly believe the majority will agree with you (use caution)
- buy-in is not necessary (use caution)
- the team will support the outcome (use caution)

Self-Assessment

Using the scale provided, rate yourself on the following leadership behaviors.

POOR   EXCELLENT

1   2   3   4   5   6   7

___ I use consensus to build buy-in and gather new ideas and perspectives.

___ I manage my emotions during the decision-making process.

___ I am clear about when I should or shouldn't make a decision.

___ I avoid the tendency to ensure perfection is reached before making a decision.

___ I publicly own my decisions.

___ I know when to stop analyzing a problem and make a decision.

Comments

_____

_____

_____

_____

_____

_____

_____

_____

_____

Action-Planning Notes

What three things in this section will help you be a better leader?

1
_____

_____

_____

2
_____

_____

_____

3
_____

_____

_____

What would change if you started or continued doing these three things?

_____

_____

_____

_____

How can you implement these changes?

_____

_____

_____

_____

Dimension 6
Delegating

"The best executive is the one who has sense enough to pick good people to do what he wants done, and self-restraint enough to keep from meddling with them while they do it."

THEODORE ROOSEVELT

Do I have a process for delegating?
Have I been successful with delegating?
Have I recognized delegating as a career enhancer?

What Is Delegating?

Delegating is assigning a task, communicating its objective and timeline, setting expectations, and providing resources and support to complete it. Delegating is a demonstration of trust in your people. It communicates that you believe that both of you can do more. It helps them grow and develop while freeing your time to address your pressing priorities. Successful delegation requires a conscious choice to share the workload and let others learn and prove themselves. This can be career enhancing for you and your people.

What it looks like:

- Explaining and confirming why the task is to be completed
- Allowing some autonomy in how the task is accomplished
- Removing barriers for the individual to be successful
- Using a structure of accountability to follow up on the task

What it is not:

- Believing your way is the only way to do it
- Giving a task without clear directions and outcomes
- Assigning only work that you do not want to do
- Giving a task to benefit only you, and not the other person

What it looks like when it is overused:

- Delegating tasks to those outside of your team
- Assigning core strategic assignments to others that you should own
- Adding unnecessary barriers to test others
- Assigning delegated tasks without regard for existing workload

When you delegate, you can drive better business and people performance. Here are some of the results you can achieve.

Business results:

- Enabling focus on your strategic priorities
- On-time delivery of key assignments
- Better support of operational and strategic goals
- Improved time management and productivity

People results:

* Professional development of your team
* Improved alignment of your team with corporate goals
* Leveraging your team's strengths
* Fostering engagement and mutual trust with your team

Coaching Tips

Preparing to Delegate

1 Analyze the project by breaking it down into basic functions and steps to determine required skills and resources.

2 Match the capabilities, personality traits, relationship skills, thinking styles, and strengths and weaknesses of your employees to the tasks you'll assign.

3 Look for members of your team who are ready for a stretch opportunity.

4 Know your own strengths and weaknesses in order to select those who complement you and to delegate the areas or tasks they will handle better than you.

5 Set measurable goals for the task and have a plan to clearly communicate these expectations, verbally and/or in writing.

6 Delegate to give your people purpose, make them feel valued, needed, and part of the group, and to establish an environment where everyone can grow and stretch.

7 Delegate to free up your time to focus on other areas—especially the "career enhancers" or strategic initiatives that are on your own boss's agenda.

Delegating Effectively

8 Use these seven simple steps:

- Explain the "what" and clarify the "why." (Verify understanding.)

- Establish and confirm checkpoints and metrics. (Share and clarify.)

- Make sure they have the needed capabilities, processes, and resources. (Arm them for the task.)

- Leave the "how" up to them. (Don't tell them how you would do it. Let them try on their own.)

- Get out of the way and let them do it. (Don't micromanage!)

- Be available for ongoing support and clarify accountability. (Don't abandon them.)

- Evaluate at completion and engage in two-way feedback. (Recognize a job well done!)

9 Clearly communicate expectations for responsibility and accountability. Ask questions to ensure they understand the project and goals.

10 Present the tasks in a way that clearly conveys your confidence in your people. They will be sensitive to this.

11 Let your people participate in setting their performance goals and areas of delegation. Give them the full story regarding budget, deadlines, resources, previous lessons learned, customer demands, and management's direction.

12 Support and encourage your people to make decisions and solve problems independently to carry out delegated tasks. Challenge them to involve you only if they have reached their limit.

13 Challenge your people to discover new ways to do their job. Inspire and support innovation.

14 Encourage those to whom you've assigned tasks to take calculated risks when appropriate.

15 Breathe new life into an existing project by delegating, allowing for new inspiration, outside perspective, brainstorming, problem solving, and creativity.

Managing Follow-Through in Delegation

16 Consider the readiness and willingness of each delegate to determine the amount of support and direction you'll provide. Have an open dialogue for maximum understanding and agreement.

17 Have contingency plans in place for high-priority delegated tasks in case a problem develops.

18 Encourage your people to give you periodic feedback on delegated projects. You cannot afford to be surprised.

19 Use questioning techniques to help them discover answers to barriers they may encounter. This is more effective than merely telling them how you would do it. Help them come up with their best answer or solution.

20 Don't assign blame too quickly if you discover the person is having difficulty. Help them analyze what went wrong, what could be improved, and what is the best course of action. Use this opportunity for valuable coaching moments to help them learn and grow.

21 Check that everyone has been given the correct tools, training, and support for the job you've asked them to do.

Overcoming Challenges to Delegation

22 If you're newly promoted, evaluate what tasks you should stop doing and what tasks you should delegate, so you can do tasks uniquely fitted for your new role.

23 Avoid the mindsets that you can do it better yourself, you can do it faster alone, you don't have time to teach others, or you want to make sure that you get the credit. If you don't delegate, you're not an effective manager.

24 Discuss poor job performance from a learning perspective, with constructive feedback.

25 Don't assume you've clearly communicated expectations and direction. Seek confirmation.

26 Don't become discouraged from delegating again when delegating ends in poor results. Rarely is a failure one-sided. Analyze why it happened and learn from it.

27 Never feel threatened by your people for doing a job better than you could.

28 Don't worry about losing some control. Have you given your delegates the clear instructions and commensurate authority to do the job? Have you established limits? Good—then turn it loose and provide support when they need it.

29 Avoid condemning new or unusual ideas.

Self-Assessment

Using the scale provided, rate yourself on the following leadership behaviors.

POOR ————————————————————————— EXCELLENT

1   2   3   4   5   6   7

___ I clearly explain the task I delegate.

___ I set measurable goals for the task I delegate.

___ I avoid completing the same task I just delegated.

___ I am available for support and feedback.

___ I adjust how I follow up on delegated tasks based on the experience of the person and the requirements of the task.

___ I use delegation to help me be more time effective.

___ I use delegation to develop others.

Comments

_____

_____

_____

_____

_____

_____

_____

_____

_____

Action-Planning Notes

What three things in this section will help you be a better leader?

1

_____

_____

_____

2

_____

_____

_____

3

_____

_____

_____

What would change if you started or continued doing these three things?

_____

_____

_____

_____

How can you implement these changes?

_____

_____

_____

Dimension 7
Dependability

"Ability is important in our quest for
success, but dependability is crucial."

ZIG ZIGLAR

Do I meet deadlines and expectations?
Do I follow through on promises?
Would my boss, co-workers, and customers say that I do?

What Is Dependability?

Dependable leaders have reputations as those who will always
come through, and their bosses know they will. Dependability is a willingness to hold oneself personally accountable and
to accomplish the assignment regardless of the obstacles. A
dependable leader is known for always delivering, even when
receiving the toughest, most closely watched tasks.

What it looks like:

- Prioritizing assignments based on schedule demands and requests

- Routinely informing others of delays as well as completion

- Committing to quality in all aspects of work

- Setting commitments and completing them every time

What it is not:

- Overcommitting and underdelivering
- Maintaining a level of minimal or poor communication
- Lacking understanding of the impact of your work on others
- Becoming an obstacle for progress or completion

What it looks like when it is overused:

- Ensuring delivery even at the expense and detriment of team members

- Showing unrealistic optimism with projects and failing to understand reality

- Excessively proclaiming to others how dependable you are

- Goal obsession so you can prove yourself to others time and time again

When you lead with dependability, you can drive better business and people performance. Here are some of the results you can achieve.

Business results:

- Increasing personal accountability and productivity
- Overcoming obstacles and achieving desired outcomes
- Consistently delivering quality
- Fostering customer trust and loyalty

People results:

* Communicating status and updates to stakeholders
* Understanding the impact of work on others
* Improving cross-functional collaboration
* Raising the bar for dependability in your work group

Coaching Tips

Habits of a Dependable Leader

1 Make it your personal policy to complete, on time, every assignment you receive.

2 Set aside five minutes at the beginning of each day to review your commitments.

3 Be proactive in recognizing what needs to be done—and do it.

4 Be punctual.

5 Look for ways to get something done rather than for reasons it can't be done.

6 To resolve a problem, identify and eliminate the root cause rather than looking for a temporary fix.

7 Focus on outcomes. You'll be judged on what you are able to deliver.

8 Do the right thing even though it is rarely the popular thing.

9 Do what you say you will do.

10 Do more than what is expected.

11 Let your own satisfaction be enough to give you the motivation you need to maintain high-quality standards of work

and job completion. Those who rely on external motivation and kudos from their boss may not always receive it. Consequently, they may lack the required motivation to get the job done well. Let it come from within.

12 Solicit feedback from your associates: What is their perception of your dependability?

13 Manage your emotions and exercise self-control: stop and think before you act. What impact will your behavior have on your team and the enterprise?

Dependability to Enhance Your Career

14 Be seen as reliable. This reputation is the best long-term self-marketing, and the most meaningful and critical tasks are usually given to the most committed people.

15 Examine your heart for commitment, motivation, dedication, and direct involvement in the organization's future. These lead to dependability that generates trusting, cooperative, productive relationships and is essential for your long-term success.

16 Meet unreasonable requirements or deadlines to stand above most everyone else and be recognized for superior performance.

17 Nourish your character by making the right choices for steady growth from day to day and year to year. Just as trees grow slowly and steadily when given proper nutrients and conditions, you will grow into—and be known as—a strong, upright individual who is guided by an inner sense of right and wrong.

18 Find out your boss's perception of the characteristics of superior performance.

19 Monitor your personal performance. It's not uncommon for an organization to "raise the bar" of its quality metrics. Stay with or exceed those levels.

20 Stay alert. Keep your antennae fully engaged. Be aware of projects, assignments, steps, phases, and elements that must be done and do them. Solicit feedback.

21 When your boss asks you to do something, don't view it as a suggestion.

Being a Dependable Leader

22 Understand the relationships that your projects have with others. This will give you a vision of the broader purpose and expand your reputation for dependability.

23 Establish genuine, appropriate, and healthy relationships with associates at all levels of the enterprise. However, avoid any impression of being self-serving or promoting your own ambitions or agendas.

24 Ask other stakeholders what their priorities are within the project. What may seem insignificant to you may be perceived as vital in the eyes of your boss, employees, or peers.

25 Look out for and suggest new ways to save your organization money. Initiate improvements that align with bigger company goals.

26 Communicate. Keep your boss informed as appropriate. Keep your people in the loop of important developments.

27 Admit your mistakes. Set a standard of honesty and be an example of not covering up errors or making excuses.

28 Run a self-diagnostic on whether you're accomplishing what's truly important. Are you delivering measurable results or just staying busy and delivering "activity"?

29 Live quality. Breathe quality. Embrace quality. Preach quality. Become a yardstick of it. It will sustain you. And others will get the message.

30 Follow through and deliver on your commitments.

31 Record action items in meetings.

Avoiding Obstacles to Dependability

32 Never let down on your level of commitment even if you feel it is not appreciated, you had a disappointing performance review, or you did not receive the bonus you were expecting. Your consistency and attitude will ultimately be recognized. At the very least, you will be true to your own high standards.

33 Don't assume that someone else got the message or that a part of the project was completed. Be proactive and follow up.

34 Avoid procrastination.

35 Don't make promises or commitments to others when you feel pressured, especially if you're not sure you can deliver.

36 Avoid the practice of committing just to be nice, and then not following through.

37 Identify how often you feel overloaded or overwhelmed: this can have a negative effect on your output.

38 Don't overcommit or make promises you can't keep.

39 Don't put off conveying negative information to your boss and senior management; you have an obligation to keep them informed. Even if it reflects poorly on you, they will most likely be more understanding and willing to work with you to solve the issue if you're up front with them. Don't dilute the message. Suggest solutions and enlist their help to tackle the problem. Your reputation of honesty will be preserved.

40 Don't let your credibility be damaged with a single foolish statement or action.

41 Don't let important details slip between the cracks.

42 If you're unable to meet a deadline or complete a project to the specifications you promised, don't waste time trying to cover it up or blame-shift. Own your mistake, then let them know what you're actively doing to fix it. Use this opportunity to illustrate your determination and commitment to tackling and solving problems.

Self-Assessment

Using the scale provided, rate yourself on the following leadership behaviors.

POOR   EXCELLENT

1   2   3   4   5   6   7

____ I consistently meet deadlines.

____ I consistently meet or exceed the expected quality of work.

____ I know my boss would say that I follow through on my commitments.

____ I know my direct reports would say that I follow through on my commitments.

____ I know my peers would say that I follow through on my commitments.

Comments

_____

_____

_____

_____

_____

_____

_____

_____

_____

_____

Action-Planning Notes

What three things in this section will help you be a better leader?

1

_____

_____

_____

2

_____

_____

_____

3

_____

_____

_____

What would change if you started or continued doing these three things?

_____

_____

_____

_____

How can you implement these changes?

_____

_____

_____

_____

Dimension 8
Focusing on Results

"The greater danger for most of us lies not in setting
our aim too high and falling short; but in
setting our aim too low, and achieving our mark."

MICHELANGELO

Do I stay focused on results during stressful situations?
Do I establish clear and realistic timelines?
Do I monitor and measure performance?

What Is Focusing on Results?

Focusing on results is the ability to target and plan a desired outcome with precision and conviction. It requires persistence to manage competing priorities, tighter schedules, higher-quality standards, and increasingly complex work at lower cost. It includes setting clear expectations for assignments, leveraging resources, and removing obstacles to employee performance. It's starting with the end in mind and working effectively with the authority and influence you have, and with all the accountability of a CEO.

What it looks like:

- Knowing, sharing, and fulfilling the organization's mission and critical initiatives

- Delivering the best value for your organization, team, and customers

- Setting milestones, managing risks, coordinating efforts, and providing updates

- Establishing performance metrics and owning personal and team consequences

What it is not:

- Confusing activity with accomplishment
- Taking on work that belongs to others
- Lacking accountability for goals and performance
- Ignoring or discounting risks

What it looks like when it is overused:

- Obsessively focusing on goal fulfillment at the expense of the rest of the business

- Believing that you are the only one who can accomplish the goal

- Exclusively focusing on business results and neglecting the people side

- Setting and never backing down from highly unrealistic expectations for others

When you focus on results, you can drive better business and people performance. Here are some of the results you can achieve.

Business results:

- Communicating clear priorities and expectations
- Delivering your best work with vision and precision
- Managing risks and competing demands
- Optimizing value for stakeholders and customers

People results:

- Removing obstacles to both employee performance and accountability

- Coordination and collaboration within and between teams

- Optimal alignment of resources for an engaged workforce

- Fostering an environment of continuous improvement

Coaching Tips

Team and Relationship Building to Focus on Results

1 Have regular face time with your staff and direct reports to learn how they are doing, what their concerns are, and what you can do to help them meet their objectives.

2 Foster a culture of continuous improvement, where everyone takes the initiative to consciously look for ways to enhance processes, systems, and transactions. Demonstrate how everyone wins by increasing quality and decreasing costs.

3 Review the roles and assignments of each of your key players. Assign the appropriate degree of authority to each one to streamline the workflow.

4 Ask yourself and your team if you both are focusing time and resources on the highest-priority items. Less important items can be tempting because they seem easier but are actually distracting from the truly critical items.

5 Identify the individuals and teams who are meeting or surpassing their targeted metrics. Have them team up with others who are struggling to share their best practices so everyone can benefit and move ahead.

6 Help your team and associates recognize the difference between long hours and actual results. Busy does not always equal accomplishment. Help them identify ways to be more efficient and productive.

7 Spend time establishing relationships across the organization to share ideas and information, test options, and optimize work. Effective collaboration is key to driving sustainable performance and results.

8 Celebrate achievement and accomplishment.

Strategies, Processes, and Metrics for Focusing on Results

9 Know the organization's critical initiatives and set your goals to support them—daily, weekly, monthly, and quarterly.

10 Identify and prioritize the needs of your customer, both internally and externally.

11 Prioritize tasks in order to do quality work while still meeting the schedule.

12 Determine the high-payoff items and focus your time on them. Learn what's truly important to your boss, your boss's boss, and senior management.

13 Keep your goals visible and review progress daily.

14 Identify the milestones in each project and focus on achieving them.

15 Set clear expectations for your people.

16 Establish and meet deadlines for yourself and your team.

17 Periodically look at the ability of your suppliers and other business partners to meet projected requirements. Probe deep to ensure you can expect their ongoing support as you grow. Test it. Be certain. Your future success depends on it.

18 Identify the critical components of your organizational strategy. Determine how each is performing and adding value to the organization's goals. Identify where each is struggling or vulnerable. Explore your processes, systems, technology, and communication flow to diagnose improvement opportunities.

19 Schedule regular process reviews to analyze and assess the organization's progress and coordinated performance. Do your shared services and business groups receive the appropriate amount of support from each other? Identify the communication stumbling blocks that impede the expected and needed results.

20 Establish a system for team communication of high-, medium-, and low-priority items.

21 Use tested and proven metrics to measure and improve all aspects of the workflow.

22 Make sure everyone has the correct tools, training, and support for the job you ask them to do.

23 Remove obstacles your people have in doing their day-to-day jobs.

24 Identify critical paths and remove obstacles.

25 Make a list of desired business results and a list of desired people results and ensure you focus on both lists (not just one or the other).

Personal Perspective, Action, and Development for Focusing on Results

26 Recognize that the higher up you go, the more you need others to help get the work done. Eagerly include others and share credit. Beware of being perceived as trying to get ahead at the expense of others. You could become the victim of sabotage.

27 Demonstrate your orientation to action through careful risk-taking, exceeding performance targets, and going beyond the expected.

28 When you make promises or commitments, be persistent to follow through and *deliver* on them. You will develop a reputation of credibility and trust.

29 Do it now. Err on taking action rather than inaction.

30 If uncertain, clarify your boss's expectations for you and your work. This will make it easier for you to deliver assigned tasks successfully.

31 Keep your boss informed on the progress of your work.

Avoiding Hindrances to Focusing on Results

32 Don't expect others to be accountable unless you are. You are the example and your behavior will be watched and judged.

33 Don't let important details slip between the cracks.

34 Don't take a purely reactive approach to business needs and problems. Constant fire drills will wear down and weaken your team, leading to burnout.

35 When your result is not the end product desired by you or your boss, analyze it fully to learn what you would do differently next time. Consider recording your findings in a personal learning journal that you can review periodically.

36 Identify and eliminate the root cause of the problem rather than looking for a temporary fix.

37 Don't disregard the politics of your environment, but be careful not to let them dominate you, your time, or your attitude.

Self-Assessment

Using the scale provided, rate yourself on the following leadership behaviors.

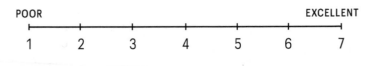

POOR   EXCELLENT

1   2   3   4   5   6   7

____ I start with the end in mind.

____ I remain focused during stressful situations.

____ I establish clear metrics to monitor and measure performance.

____ I establish clear and realistic timelines.

____ I establish agreed upon roles and responsibilities.

____ I establish agreed upon deliverables.

____ I hold others accountable.

____ I hold myself accountable.

Comments

_____

_____

_____

_____

_____

_____

_____

_____

Action-Planning Notes

What three things in this section will help you be a better leader?

1

2

3

What would change if you started or continued doing these three things?

How can you implement these changes?

Dimension 9
Personal Integrity

"What lies behind us and what lies before us are tiny matters compared to what lies within us."

RALPH WALDO EMERSON

Does my walk match my talk?

Do I consider the ethical implications before making a decision?

Do I treat people with dignity and respect?

What Is Personal Integrity?

Personal integrity is demonstrating consistent honesty and commitment to your word. It's following through to deliver on what you say you will do. It's exhibiting principled leadership and sound business ethics, thereby earning the trust of others.

Personal integrity is being authentic, being true to your values, and honoring the goodness in others. As a leader, your single most important attribute is being trusted.

What it looks like:

- Taking responsibility for actions and results

- Committing to a positive value set and living according to it

- Placing fairness and honesty above other outcomes

- Treating others with dignity and respect—as people and not objects

What it is not:

- Allowing the end to justify the means

- Building fear instead of trust

- Thinking what you say is more important than what you do

- Compromising your reputation with a single impulsive decision

What it looks like when it is overused:

- Taking all the heat and repeatedly covering the mistakes of others

- Being unwilling to compromise at any time

- Being so careful about preserving your reputation that it prevents needed action

- Being so literal in your interpretation of rules and not allowing reasonable variability

With personal integrity, you can drive better business and people performance. Here are some of the results you can achieve.

Business results:

- Supporting your organization's good reputation
- Delivering ethical business decisions
- Eliminating legally suspect behavior and minimizing risk
- Fostering stakeholder and customer trust

People results:

- Building a strong personal reputation for honesty
- Helping others feel respected and valued
- Fostering an environment of trust and openness
- Creating high ethical standards for your team

Coaching Tips

Communicating with Personal Integrity

1 Establish the norm of honest, open communication with employees, customers, vendors, and all stakeholders. This will directly contribute to an environment of trust.

2 Use clear, unambiguous wording to avoid the possibility of unintended promises and commitments being read into your statements.

3 When challenged or questioned, give straightforward, complete, honest answers. Evasive replies will catch up to you and damage your credibility and integrity.

4 Preserve your reputation of honesty by conveying negative information promptly and candidly to your boss and senior management. You have an obligation to keep them informed on issues that are important to them—even if it reflects poorly on you.

5 Speak to your team and associates in their work areas to find out what their values are. You can also share yours with them to discover and leverage commonalities.

6 Ask trusted associates their opinion of your trustworthiness and honesty. Listen openly to them without rationalizing.

7 Encourage open and honest discussions about ethical issues as they surface.

8 As an important step to building trust, sincerely listen to others to learn what they are thinking and how they feel.

9 Tell the full truth quickly while being sensitive to language that could hurt others.

10 Maintain personal control if you find yourself in a hostile or emotionally charged situation. Respond with respect and professionalism. Take deep breaths, gather your thoughts, and offer language and body language that will defuse rather than escalate the situation. The test will be whether you later regret your behavior.

11 When you're trying to reestablish trust, learn from those who've done this successfully. Profit from their experience and put it into practice if it fits your situation.

12 Never post or share anything online that you would not mind having on the front page of a newspaper.

Leading with Personal Integrity

13 Read your organization's code of values or ethics. Learn it; be true to it; teach it to others. Model it in all your transactions. Encourage others to do the same. If your organization doesn't have a code of values, start one.

14 Seek advice from your firm's ethics officer or ombudsman.

15 Create an environment in which people are comfortable coming to you with their concerns. *Honor their confidence.* Your people's and superiors' confidence and trust in you are absolutely essential for you to succeed!

16 Protect the interests of others to earn their respect and trust; let your direct reports and teammates know how much you value and welcome feedback on how you can improve in any aspect of your job. This will let you know what you are doing well and what you can improve on.

17 Create an environment of trust, transparency, and respect with your customers.

18 Don't be too anxious to make the sale—you may overpromise.

19 Do the right thing even if it's not the popular thing.

20 Actively help your organization reestablish its reputation after a trying situation or period.

21 Do what you say you will do. Deliver on your commitments.

22 Think through and list some of your best intentions over the past week or month. Note how many of them happened. What stopped you from following through on any? What can you do differently so your good intentions materialize as actions?

23 Ask yourself these questions when facing a tough ethical dilemma:

- Would I hurt the reputation of another?

- Would I destroy the trust I've tried so hard to establish?

- What would my mother say?

- Would it be fair to all parties?

- How would I feel about myself?

- How would I explain my actions to my family?

- What counsel would I give someone else facing this situation?

24 Build a reputation of trust. This isn't based on a single event or moment. It's influenced by a series of interactions, behaviors, and experiences—all observed by others who gradually formulate the perception of trust and honesty. Without trust, it doesn't matter how brilliant, competent, talented, or skilled you are.

Setting an Example with Personal Integrity

25 Model your ethical beliefs and values with your behavior.

26 Make promises only if you truly plan (and are able) to keep them. People will remember and hold you to them. Keep track of promises and commitments (implied or direct) that you make. Monitor them. Your follow-through will directly influence others' trust in your future promises and commitments.

27 Own your mistakes without blaming others. By acknowledging them, you'll set a standard of honesty and not covering up errors or making excuses.

28 Ensure consistency between your words and actions. Hypocrisy is very damaging.

29 Treat everyone you encounter with respect and professionalism. You'll never regret it. You will, however, regret hasty judgments, gossip, and acting with superiority. And that behavior will eventually catch up to you.

30 Be alert to situations in which others are negatively discussed when they're not present. Stand up for them when

you know it's not accurate or true. Protect their reputations by defending them, as you would hope others would do for you if you were in their situation.

31 Prove to others that you care more about the end result than about your own image by holding yourself accountable. People will remember how you resolved a problem more than they will remember how it came about in the first place.

Avoiding Hindrances to Personal Integrity

32 Don't withhold information that your team needs. Keep them current and fully informed.

33 Don't be tempted to put a personal spin on the facts to promote your reputation or serve your own advancement. People catch on to this behavior and will begin to doubt your veracity.

34 Don't appear to know everything. This behavior leads to skepticism in others.

35 Don't let inaction on your part in addressing an unethical situation create the impression that you and your department or organization condone such behavior.

36 Don't show deferential treatment based on someone's professional status. Others can observe a lot about your character and how you will eventually treat them by how you address or acknowledge the cleaning crew as compared to the CEO.

37 Resist making commitments to others just to placate them. If you do, and you don't stay true to them, your reputation and integrity will be damaged.

38 Don't burn bridges. It's very likely you'll be forced to rebuild them in the future.

Self-Assessment

Using the scale provided, rate yourself on the following leadership behaviors.

POOR   EXCELLENT

1   2   3   4   5   6   7

____ I do what I say.

____ I consider ethical implications before making a business decision.

____ I privately support issues/decisions I support in public.

____ I advise others to remain true to their values.

____ I model the values of the organization.

Comments

_____

_____

_____

_____

_____

_____

_____

_____

_____

_____

_____

_____

_____

Action-Planning Notes

What three things in this section will help you be a better leader?

1

_____

_____

_____

2

_____

_____

_____

3

_____

_____

_____

What would change if you started or continued doing these three things?

_____

_____

_____

_____

How can you implement these changes?

_____

_____

_____

_____

Dimension 10
Problem Solving

"The significant problems we have
cannot be solved at the same level of
thinking with which we created them."

ALBERT EINSTEIN

Do I look for root causes of problems?
Do I encourage others to express differing views?
Do I define desired outcomes and an implementation plan?

What Is Problem Solving?

Problem solving is the ability to define and analyze a root issue and desired outcome to generate a high-quality solution with appropriate buy-in. It requires prioritizing problems effectively. It involves breaking down difficult or undefined issues into manageable steps, using a systematic approach, on schedule and within budget. It leverages cross-functional, multilevel brainstorming and perspectives or ideas to define the true, core issue, optimize and implement the solution, and follow through for continuous improvement.

What it looks like:

* Defining the problem and desired outcomes

* Researching and analyzing influencing factors that lead to root causes

* Identifying realistic tactics and timelines

* Balancing and incorporating multiple, varied perspectives

What it is not:

* Overlooking relevant people and resources in the process

* Addressing a symptom rather than the core issue

* Neglecting to use a systematic problem-solving process or approach

* Ignoring the "little things" before they become big problems

What it looks like when it is overused:

* Applying the same approach to solve every problem
* Not knowing when "good enough" is a sufficient answer
* Valuing each voice or stakeholder equally
* Creating excessive contingencies and possible scenarios

When you solve problems effectively, you can drive better business and people performance. Here are some of the results you can achieve.

Business results:

- Revealing root causes to discuss and resolve deeper issues

- Implementing solutions that support both customers and stakeholders

- Matching priorities with available time, resources, and business impact

- Revising processes for continuous improvement

People results:

- Creating needed buy-in for a solution
- Promoting fresh, diverse thoughts and ideas
- Collaborating cross-functionally and at all professional levels
- Fostering a creative, inclusive culture

Coaching Tips

First Steps to Defining and Solving a Problem

1 Note the typical steps in a problem-solving cycle:

- Defining the problem based on root cause
- Generating solutions
- Selecting a solution
- Implementing the solution
- Evaluating the implementation
- Improving continually

2 Begin to define the root cause of the problem by getting multiple perspectives on it: ask each team member to state the problem as they see it—in their own words.

3 List all related aspects of the problem by topic: symptoms, directly related, result of, implications. This will help you sort out relevant causes.

4 Avoid assumptions. Define the relevant facts and have your team test them carefully as facts—not assumptions that have crept into the fact column.

5 If you and your team are too close to the problem to see and understand it properly, seek outside help to provide a fresh, objective perspective.

6 Consider how other stakeholders would view the problem. Look at it from the viewpoint of customers, vendors, your boss and boss's boss, internal customers, and other associates. When appropriate, ask them for their thoughts.

7 Make sure the problem you've identified is not really a symptom. The first and most critical step in problem solving is accurately defining the problem. Peter Drucker's statement is on target: "A problem well defined is a problem half-solved."

8 Once the initial issue is well defined, have the team break it down into smaller problem areas that seem to be the highest-priority items, factoring in what your customer values.

Accurately Solving the Problem

9 Bring together a brainstorming and problem-solving group of five to eight people of varied backgrounds, with both logical and creative mindsets. Involve at least one who operates closest to the root issue daily, for a unique, front-row perspective.

10 Place the problem definition on a whiteboard so your team can see it during the problem-solving process.

11 Establish an atmosphere of "anything goes," with no criticism or evaluation (verbal or nonverbal) of any suggestion that is brought forward. Once the brainstorming ends, critiquing begins.

12 Identify where you are today and where you want to be (your end result) once the problem is resolved. This gap will help direct your approach and keep you on track.

13 Have your team look at the history of the problem. Review how it's been dealt with in the past. Consider the culture and norms that have shaped the current situation.

14 Use all available tools, forms, data, metrics, and official or unofficial input to help identify possible solutions. Don't overlook or ignore anything.

15 Consider using the Janusian approach (named for Janus, the Roman god of beginnings and endings—whose head appears on both sides of Roman coins). You merely ask two sets of questions:

Set 1:

* Who is most likely to respond to this situation?

* How has the situation been addressed in the past?

* Which tools and processes have been used to address similar problems?

Set 2 asks the opposite:

* Who is *least* likely to respond to this situation?

* How has this situation *not* been addressed in the past?

* What tools and processes have *not* been used to address similar problems?

You'll be amazed by how limiting your approach has been using Set 1 questions, and how mind-expanding Set 2 questions can be.

16 Another way to look at problem solving is to take one of these two approaches (or a combination):

- Convergent—a logical and deliberate path leading toward a solution

- Divergent—a more creative approach relying on intuition, humor, absurdity, and innovation

17 Embrace creativity. Think outside the norm.

18 Share the problem with someone who has no part in the process. They will look at it with complete objectivity and a fresh perspective. Share their input with the team.

19 Seek solutions from unlikely sources, such as young or inexperienced team members, not only from seasoned leaders.

20 Continue the analysis and brainstorming process to select the right solution balancing optimal value for customers and stakeholders with time, budget, and resource constraints.

Final Steps to Solving a Problem

21 Check to be sure you haven't entered the process with a predetermined solution in mind. Be open to the input of others as you and your team make a final decision.

22 Create a rough implementation plan as part of your solution; it will help you determine feasibility for moving forward. This would be a perfect time to get feedback from outside objective associates, especially those who would be part of a cross-functional implementation team. You may need to rethink various aspects.

23 When your team is completely ready to present their solution to senior management, first consider trying it out on one or two executives who support your efforts yet are independent enough to give you honest feedback. They bring real-world reactions to you and are providing you a huge service. Seriously consider their viewpoints and don't be discouraged if you need to rethink the solution.

24 Identify the three major barriers that might prevent a successful implementation. Develop contingency plans to address and minimize these barriers.

25 When you're sure it's the right solution, implement it! Examine: 1) available resources, 2) who and what will be impacted, and 3) potential resistance and reasons for it. Build your messaging to maximize buy-in, communicate it, and follow through.

26 Plan check-in points to evaluate the implementation.

27 Be prepared for improvements and tweaks along the way.

28 Moving forward, keep your eyes on red flags and "little things" to resolve them before they become big problems.

Avoiding Hindrances to Problem Solving

29 Face the problem head-on. Don't rationalize it away. Involve a relevant and interested team, and solve it. If you avoid it, a magic wand won't take it away. Instead of magically disappearing, it usually becomes worse.

30 Define the true root issue from the beginning. If you're spinning your wheels trying to resolve a non-issue, you'll waste even more time and generate even more confusion and frustration.

31 Don't ignore your gut instinct, suspicions, and unexpected or illogical ideas. Keep a separate list of these. They often pay off in some way and to some degree.

32 Don't let current pressure from budgets, schedules, senior management, media, and so on limit or restrict your vision of the real cause(s) of your problem. Imagine a situation in which you're free of these pressures. How would you then see your problem, issue, or concern?

33 Separate the problem from the person(s) who caused it. The blame game wastes time and causes resentment and other negative feelings.

34 Don't let the usual talkative team members dominate; allow the quieter ones a chance to chime in. Involve every member of the group by asking them to express their views, ideas, opinions, and skepticism about the issue being debated.

35 Don't stop at the first right answer. You'll likely generate multiple possible solutions.

Self-Assessment

Using the scale provided, rate yourself on the following leadership behaviors.

POOR   EXCELLENT

1   2   3   4   5   6   7

____ I clearly identify and define a problem.
____ I obtain multiple perspectives when identifying a problem.
____ I look to see how others have addressed a similar problem.
____ I consider multiple methods on how to solve a problem.
____ I prioritize problems effectively.
____ I effectively manage people in addressing problems.
____ I continually seek to improve a solution.

Comments

_____
_____
_____
_____
_____
_____
_____
_____
_____
_____
_____
_____
_____

Action-Planning Notes

What three things in this section will help you be a better leader?

1

_____
_____
_____

2

_____
_____
_____

3

_____
_____
_____

What would change if you started or continued doing these three things?

_____
_____
_____
_____

How can you implement these changes?

_____
_____
_____
_____

QUADRANT III
DEVELOP SELF
& OTHERS

Dimension 11
Coaching

"A bit of fragrance always clings
to the hand that gives you roses."

CHINESE PROVERB

Do I help employees improve their performance?
Do I give timely and specific improvement feedback?
Do I provide needed training?

What Is Coaching?

Coaching is guiding and challenging an individual to achieve improved performance through self-discovery, feedback, encouragement, and skill development. A leader is accountable to both employees and the organization for developing and growing people so they can perform at their full potential and achieve job satisfaction. Coaching helps build a person's strengths and identifies ways to manage personal challenges and opportunities. Effective leaders have a coaching style that shows care and concern for the individual, builds engagement, fosters open dialogue, and encourages diversity of thought.

What it looks like:

* Matching employee ability and attitude with assignments

* Providing in-the-moment feedback, formal coaching, and training

* Supporting individuals to own their development and performance

* Creating an environment of support and self-discovery

What it is not:

* Thinking mistakes are grounds for failure

* Telling more often than asking and listening

* Expecting people will self-develop without support

* Withholding feedback or delivering feedback in general terms only

What it looks like when it is overused:

* Using coaching during crisis or highly urgent situations

* Always favoring the other person's perspective over your own

* Using a coaching approach with inexperienced employees

* Checking in on someone's development so often it becomes smothering

With effective coaching, you can drive better business and people performance. Here are some of the results you can achieve.

Business results:

* Elevating individual and team performance
* Increasing personal ownership of customer deliverables
* Encouraging creativity and innovation
* Improving succession planning

People results:

* Increasing confidence and motivation through self-discovery

* Fostering an environment of timely feedback and dialogue

* Stretching people's abilities to achieve genuine personal growth

* Building capability for current and future assignments

Coaching Tips

Coaching Effectively

1 Focus on your employee's actual behavior, not your perception or interpretation of it.

2 Let your people know you want to help them discover opportunities for additional challenges and satisfaction. This will help you earn their hearts and minds, not just their hands, to cultivate a positive organization culture and engaged workforce.

3 Communicate confidence in the capability and potential of your direct reports and teammates. Reinforce it through delegating to them and coaching them to greater possibilities.

4 Pay attention to the receptivity level of those being coached and adapt your coaching style to best connect with them.

5 Ask more questions during coaching sessions rather than telling them the answers.

6 Set clear performance expectations, and tie specific, frequent feedback to established goals.

7 Encourage your people to develop new attitudes toward risk. This can apply to current opportunities, future prospects, and stretch assignments. Help them see that their willingness to try something will often lead to unexpected possibilities.

8 Develop and use a healthy sense of humor. It has a huge positive effect on others.

9 Take advantage of spontaneous, coachable moments.

10 Treat every issue or problem as an opportunity for learning, growth, and progress.

11 Give people options and choices—it is empowering.

12 Help your people discover and address their blind spots.

13 Provide 360-degree assessment or feedback counseling for higher-level performers to help them know their strengths and deficiencies. Help them focus on and build their strengths and improve on or compensate for their weaknesses.

Career Coaching

14 Encourage the positive performer to learn more about the job descriptions, actual job duties, requirements, and responsibilities of desirable future positions.

15 Tailor career coaching to mesh with the potential you see in your employees to be successful in their targeted areas.

16 Encourage your people to try things they normally would not try, and provide emotional support. This is especially worthwhile when they have shown greater potential or propensities toward a particular area.

17 Encourage your people not to become overpowered or intimidated by what they don't know.

18 Use career coaching to support succession planning and strengthen your organization's bench strength.

Corrective Coaching

19 Address poor or unacceptable performance right away. Bad news doesn't get better with age.

20 Focus on your employee's actual behavior, not your perception or interpretation of it.

21 Remind them of how much you value them.

22 Be specific in letting others know exactly what they did and why it is unacceptable.

23 Employ coaching when you believe the deficiency is correctable, the person has the capacity to do the work properly, and the person wants to improve.

24 Allow them reasonable time to settle into a new position.

25 Draw out their opinions of why their work or skill levels are weak. Then probe for causes and reasons.

26 Ask them what they can do specifically to avoid repeating the behavior in the future.

27 Have follow-up meetings to monitor results. Hold them accountable once performance standards are made clear.

28 Be available to them for future help.

29 For senior managers who are obviously deficient in an area they cannot remedy, consider adding a person to the team with a strength that will compensate.

30 Document performance discussions.

Coaching Precautions

31 Since performance feedback can be uncomfortable and difficult for everyone, take a positive, constructive approach: focus on improving actual behaviors and clarify that your goal is to help your employee succeed.

32 Build an environment in which risk-taking is encouraged instead of immediately rejected and condemned.

33 Don't reprimand publicly; it's the easiest way to strip someone's dignity.

34 Separate the person from the act. Correct the action, but reinforce the person.

35 Don't keep reminding them of their mistakes or shortcomings.

36 Give your employees the opportunity to stick their necks out without getting "whacked." Let them suggest improvements. Avoid condemning new or unusual ideas.

37 Examine the level of trust between you and your team. Trust requires an ongoing investment of time, patience, and interest. When there is mutual trust, there will be quality performance.

38 Consider the amount of time you spend with each of your people. Do you listen to them? Do you support them as they face new and tough assignments? Not everyone will respond the same way. Each deserves to be treated as an individual.

39 Don't spend so much time coaching low performers that your star performers feel neglected.

Self-Assessment

Using the scale provided, rate yourself on the following leadership behaviors.

POOR   EXCELLENT

1   2   3   4   5   6   7

____ I am an effective coach in helping employees improve their performance.

____ I give feedback specifically, professionally, and in a timely manner.

____ I make certain that people receive necessary and timely training and development.

____ I help employees develop, recognize, and appreciate a strong sense of personal accomplishment.

____ I have a flexible management style for a variety of challenges and people.

Comments

_____

_____

_____

_____

_____

_____

_____

_____

Action-Planning Notes

What three things in this section will help you be a better leader?

1

_____

_____

_____

2

_____

_____

_____

3

_____

_____

_____

What would change if you started or continued doing these three things?

_____

_____

_____

_____

How can you implement these changes?

_____

_____

_____

_____

Dimension 12
Ego Management

> "Of all manifestations of power,
> restraint impresses [people] most."

THUCYDIDES

Do I admit when I am wrong?
Do I pursue what is best for the team?
Do I welcome the ideas of others?

What Is Ego Management?

Ego management is having a balanced level of confidence in your own skills, tools, judgment, and experience. A strong, confident ego is needed to handle the challenges of life. Ego management combines humility and modesty with strong inner conviction and determination. Overinflated egos can hamper good decision making by shutting out the ideas of others, masking personal development needs, and generating organizational dysfunctions. And underinflated egos can deny the value you can and should add to your team and organization. The challenge is to manage your ego so it doesn't manage you!

What it looks like:

* Giving credit where it is due

* Leading the applause for your people

* Pursuing what is best for the team

* Allowing the team freedom in how they achieve the result

What it is not:

* Demeaning or belittling others

* Allowing emotions and desire for power or control to determine actions

* Making sure everyone knows how important the leader is

* Wanting others to conform to the leader on all issues

What it looks like when it is overused:

* Believing that in the end, you are always the reason for the team's success

* Never questioning or backing down from your own optimism

* Allowing louder or more dominant voices to always prevail

* Consistently doubting and not voicing your own ideas

When you manage your ego, you can drive better business and people performance. Here are some of the results you can achieve.

Business results:

- Fostering a culture of collaboration and new ideas
- Promoting good team decision making
- Improving problem solving
- Optimizing team engagement and productivity

People results:

- Allowing people the freedom to take risks
- Building personal resilience
- Professional development of leaders and staff
- Fostering trusting relationships

Coaching Tips

Managing Your Ego

1 Control your temper and emotions in times of stress and pressure. This is when the ugly part of the ego can break loose and control your interactions with others, usually causing regret later on.

2 Avoid being defensive when you learn of areas where you need to improve. Do you justify or rationalize? Or do you try to understand and apply the feedback to make needed changes?

3 Reflect on the degree of compassion or empathy you have for others. Good ego management requires that you "feel" for those who are struggling with an assignment or personal challenge and offer help or advice.

4 Slow your reaction time; reflect on self-based motives before speaking or deciding.

5 Be cautious about favoring certain employees with your time.

6 Avoid sarcasm and put-downs—in public and private.

7 Ask yourself: "How often do I look for ways to point out others who've helped me and include them in it? How often do I simply take full credit (when it is not due)?"

8 Leverage and respect the strengths of each team member.

9 Let go of the idea that you need to be the smartest person in the room. Ask a trusted associate if you appear to have a need to demonstrate to others that you're more intelligent than they are. Be aware and resist the human tendency to add your two cents to each discussion.

10 In problem-solving settings, don't be the first to offer an opinion. Let others do so. Recognize and acknowledge their input. Point out the merits of their contributions. As you express your views, be careful to not make your ideas the only right answer.

11 Avoid dominating conversations.

12 Learn to ask, "What do you think?" It will make people feel of greater value while decreasing the chance of their perception that you have an overinflated ego.

13 As you develop your team, keep in mind your own strengths and weaknesses. Select those who complement you. Delegate tasks that they will do better than you will.

14 Share positive feedback with others on a regular basis. Share the credit. Share the spotlight. Lead the applause for others.

15 Take the high road by admitting when you are wrong, and not blaming others or past events. Don't believe the lie that making a mistake makes you a bad leader. ·

Transitioning from Low to Strong Ego

16 Identify times when you discount and hold back your own opinions. Your voice matters and needs to be heard.

17 When you receive feedback, remember that you have a choice to act on it or not. Consciously decide when to listen and act on feedback from others instead of automatically reacting to every piece of feedback you hear.

18 Keep a tally when you are silent in meetings. Identify who is in those meetings or what the topics are that are discussed. Identify ways to make an appropriate impact in those meetings.

19 Write down the perceptions you think others have about you or the thoughts others might be thinking about you. Then identify why you think they might be thinking this. Ask yourself how much these perceptions matter as you seek to achieve business and people results.

20 As you ask your team, "What do you think?" ensure that you also share your own opinion in the process, especially regarding topics on which you have additional insights or organizational knowledge.

21 To increase your confidence, identify ways to help you process and prepare for conversations and meetings. Think through steps to help you feel empowered when you enter into conversations.

22 Be aware how often you share positive comments and also critical ones. If your comments are always positive, introduce constructive or critical ones to challenge thinking and behavior.

Benefits of a Healthy Ego

23 Be resilient. The ability to bounce back is another character-istic of a healthy ego. Following a major disappointment or defeat, the well-balanced ego (more humble now) learns from the experience and tries again.

24 Know that you don't have a monopoly on truth. A well-managed ego welcomes participation from others.

25 Be adaptable to change. Ego-driven people want the world to conform to them. Well-managed egos adapt to new rules, norms, and requirements.

26 Direct effort and goals toward a united purpose. When you sacrifice personal recognition for the team's performance, your shared achievements improve exponentially.

27 Don't always feel that you have to be the one to make every decision. Delegate to empower your team and free your time for your other priorities.

28 Accept responsibility for your own actions and those of your team. This encourages your team to follow in your steps and creates an environment of respect and trust.

Steps to a Healthy Ego

29 Improve your listening skills by rephrasing what you heard.

30 Think what is best for the company, the customer, and the team—not just for yourself.

31 Look back over your successes. Honestly consider how the help you received from others contributed to your achievements.

32 Make it a daily practice to willingly express gratitude, and constantly be looking for opportunities to do so.

33 Don't take yourself too seriously. Laugh more.

34 Observe others in your organization, especially senior managers and executives. Notice the way they manage their egos (either poorly or well). Then study how others react to them because of it.

35 Be genuinely courteous to everyone.

36 Support the good decisions of others, even when they don't coincide with yours.

37 Recognize that even if you're right, you may not be successful without other people's involvement and ideas.

38 Treat others as equal partners.

39 Ask for formal and informal feedback from others; consider it without rationalizing.

40 Create a personal bond by using a person's first name often in conversation. This reinforces the personal relationship rather than that of boss/subordinate.

41 Identify opportunities and ways you can "catch" others doing something well; be quick to point out and praise their successes.

42 Celebrate others' successes, and be humble about your own.

Self-Assessment

Using the scale provided, rate yourself on the following leadership behaviors.

POOR   EXCELLENT

1   2   3   4   5   6   7

____ I ask others, "What do you think?"

____ I compliment others on their efforts and accomplishments.

____ I give credit where credit is due.

____ I treat others as equals.

____ I don't dominate conversations.

____ I share the spotlight.

____ I ask for feedback and welcome it.

Comments

_____

_____

_____

_____

_____

_____

_____

_____

_____

_____

Action-Planning Notes

What three things in this section will help you be a better leader?

1
_____
_____
_____

2
_____
_____
_____

3
_____
_____
_____

What would change if you started or continued doing these three things?

_____
_____
_____
_____

How can you implement these changes?

_____
_____
_____
_____

Dimension 13
Listening

"The courage to speak must be
matched by the wisdom to listen."

ANONYMOUS

Do I maintain my focus on the current conversation?
Do I ask questions to promote understanding?
Do I observe and respond to nonverbal communication?

What Is Listening?

Listening is the ability to understand the intended message
while having an awareness of the attitudes and feelings of
others. Successful listening tunes in to verbal and nonverbal
expressions. Sincere listening sends an undeniable message
to others that you care about them, their ideas, and their
contributions. Good listening skills are essential to building

trusting, productive relationships with employees, customers, and stakeholders.

What it looks like:

* Demonstrating genuine intent to understand
* Physically turning your body and attention toward the other person
* Repeating or paraphrasing to ensure comprehension
* Asking questions to ensure clarification

What it is not:

* Faking listening while the other person is talking
* Ignoring nonverbal cues as you listen
* Preparing your reply while the person is still talking
* Letting your mind wander during the conversation

What it looks like when it is overused:

* Using silence to embarrass or intimidate others
* Repeating back statements in a condescending manner
* Passively withholding your own opinions in a conversation or meeting
* Allowing others to endlessly vent every time they speak with you

When you listen effectively, you can drive better business and people performance. Here are some of the results you can achieve.

Business results:

- Being open to new ideas
- Fostering innovation of products, services, processes
- Hearing feedback from stakeholders during times of change
- Building understanding, engagement, and commitment

People results:

- Showing you value diversity of thought and action
- Having others feel heard and valued
- Effectively reading the room
- Maintaining better working relationships

Coaching Tips

Preparing for Effective Listening

1 Clear your mind of distractions prior to engaging in a conversation.

2 Remove physical barriers—don't sit behind your desk or workstation.

3 Turn off your phone and put it away. Don't allow any distraction to divert your attention from what's truly important— listening to your associate. Show them courtesy, respect, and a sincere interest in what they have to say.

4 Use techniques to remind you to watch more as you listen. For instance, if you keep your eyes focused on their face, this will help you avoid distractions while you look for important nonverbal cues and emotions revealed in their eyes and facial expressions.

5 Avoid unhelpful nonverbal cues. Don't cross your arms, as this can signal being tuned out. Restless motions can

indicate boredom. Eyes looking to the side may signal your attention is being drawn away by something or someone else. Tapping a pen denotes nervousness or lack of interest.

6 Make it your mission to be empathetic to others. Put yourself in their shoes to understand where they're coming from and what they're really trying to say.

7 Be aware of your own filters (emotions, biases, assumptions).

8 Listen without judgment.

9 Listen to understand, not to respond. Don't form rebuttals while the other person is speaking. Remain silent when appropriate—don't interrupt.

10 Refrain from automatically solving the person's problem. Often they just need to be heard.

Interactive Listening

11 Follow these overall steps for effective listening:

- Search for common ground.

- Keep an open mind.

- Be interested and attentive.

- Don't give advice.

- Give nonverbal acknowledgments (head nod, eye contact, facial expression, smile).

12 Listen with your ears *and* your eyes. Research reveals that 80 percent or more of communication is nonverbal. Only 20 percent consists of the spoken word. (Nonverbal includes posture and body language, eyes, tone, facial expressions, intensity, energy, clothing, atmosphere, mood, etc.)

13 In addition to listening with your ears and eyes, use your mouth to listen. This is called "active listening"—verbally mirroring what the other person has expressed to show you're listening, check your understanding, and remember what they said. To excel at active listening:

- Suspend your own judgments or reactions in order to focus on and clarify the other person's thoughts and feelings.

- Occasionally restate or summarize by paraphrasing what you think the person said.

- Ask clarifying questions.

- Encourage with positive prompting for more information.

- Reflect on their motivations or feelings.

- Probe with questions.

- Give feedback.

- Seek confirmation.

14 To repeat back key thoughts or ideas, say, "Let me make sure I understand what you are saying. I believe you said..." This will allow them to confirm that you do get it or give them the opportunity to clarify.

15 Ask open-ended clarifying questions—what do you mean; why do you feel that way; why do you say that; could you elaborate on that; how so; what happened next; what I hear you saying is; how do you feel about that. This will help to ensure you've understood while letting the speaker know you sincerely want to understand.

16 Make a strong impression in the meeting by writing down their key points. Convey to them with this simple action

that you really want to remember what they've said because it's important to you.

17 Be aware that the speaker will also be watching for how you listen. Respond with your own nonverbal behaviors: nodding when you agree, facing them, leaning forward when seated, smiling and acknowledging their emotions when appropriate.

Listening in Specific Situations

18 During brainstorming sessions, make sure others do more talking than you do. If you're the leader, don't voice your opinion until all others have stated theirs.

19 When listening to your boss, try to identify their agenda, hot buttons, stresses, concerns, and objectives. This will provide better context for the conversation and help you understand how and when to respond.

20 Be particularly attentive in times of conflict. These critical moments require that you be tuned in to every cue, signal, nuance, gesture, hesitation, and emotion. Watch their faces and eyes; listen for tone and pitch changes; study inflections and reactions.

21 Before agreeing to make an appointment when an associate requests time to discuss an important or critical issue, make sure you'll be free to give them your complete attention during the meeting. If your schedule changes, reschedule for a time when you'll be able to provide your full attention—and keep the meeting.

22 When there's disagreement, recognize that understanding and agreeing are not the same thing. Try diligently to see their perspective, and don't worry that your sincere

attempt to understand them will give the appearance of agreement. You need to see their point of view to better relate. They need to know you understand their point of view. The understanding is imperative, while always agreeing with them is not.

Benefits of Listening

23 Be a better listener to increase your control of the situation.

24 Listen with genuine intent to let others know you truly care about them and their concerns. People don't care how much you know until they know how much you care.

25 Learn to recognize the filters (biases, emotions, prejudices, assumptions) of your boss, each of your employees, and peers. This will help you understand them and identify your own filters.

26 Sincerely listen to others to learn what they are thinking and how they feel; this is often the first step to building trust.

27 Invite your people to bring you their problems so they feel you are in touch, that you want to listen to them. Your job isn't to solve their problems but instead to listen and give them guidance and support, while letting them own their problems.

28 Listen regularly to people one-on-one to earn their hearts and minds, not just their hands, to foster morale and improve productivity.

29 Use reflective listening to help you understand the problem while guiding them to resolve it on their own. Listen to the problem, then "reflect" it back to them, to check understanding. This shows you care enough to hear them and trust them enough to resolve it independently.

Self-Assessment

Using the scale provided, rate yourself on the following leadership behaviors.

POOR   EXCELLENT

| 1 | 2 | 3 | 4 | 5 | 6 | 7 |

____ I suspend judgment when listening to others.
____ I keep eye contact with others when listening.
____ I pay attention to their nonverbal cues.
____ I ask questions without having predetermined solutions.
____ I rephrase their comments to ensure understanding.

Comments

_____
_____
_____
_____
_____
_____
_____
_____
_____
_____
_____
_____
_____
_____
_____
_____
_____

Action-Planning Notes

What three things in this section will help you be a better leader?

1
_____
_____
_____

2
_____
_____
_____

3
_____
_____
_____

What would change if you started or continued doing these three things?

_____
_____
_____
_____

How can you implement these changes?

_____
_____
_____
_____

Dimension 14
Personal Development

"The unexamined life
is not worth living."

SOCRATES

Am I open to feedback and adaptable to change?
Do I know my strengths?
Do I apply new tools and learning in my job?

What Is Personal Development?

Personal development is the ongoing pursuit of improving
your abilities and knowledge. It requires staying up-to-date
on trends and best practices to remain relevant and effective.
It involves a strong personal network to learn from the ideas
and experiences of others. It's leveraging positive and negative experiences to improve personal and team effectiveness.

Personal development for yourself and your team is an essential part of career planning, advancement, and management.

What it looks like:

- Becoming aware of how you are perceived by others
- Adapting and learning new skills and techniques
- Seeking the support and encouragement of others
- Applying new skills to current and new situations

What it is not:

- Lacking awareness of behavioral blind spots that can derail your career

- Ignoring improvement suggestions from colleagues

- Ignoring personal feedback from performance assessments and reviews

- Getting into day-to-day ruts that close doors on future opportunities

What it looks like when it is overused:

- Repeatedly embracing the next big thing and dropping other ideas just because they aren't

- Conducting self-reflection so often, you overthink your development needs

- Collecting books, binders, and conference lanyards as if they were awards to display instead of ideas and tools to be used

- Expecting self-improvement to happen quicker than is realistic

Through personal development, you can drive better business and people performance. Here are some of the results you can achieve.

Business results:

- Personal and business agility
- Leveraging trends and best practices for better performance
- Improving and innovating products and services
- Anticipating market and customer needs

People results:

- Building the talent pipeline through networking
- Promoting a culture of development
- Being open to positive, constructive feedback
- Improving engagement and productivity

Coaching Tips

Self-Assessment for Personal Development

1 Assess your current capabilities. Identify where you'd like to be in five years. What will that require? Now define the gap between where you are and where you'd like to be. This becomes your starting point for your personal development.

2 Review your current job requirements. Which parts do you enjoy the most and least, and why? This can help you with setting your career and development goals.

3 Assess how flexible you are. One of the biggest career stoppers is being unable to adapt to differences and changes.

4 Determine whether your personal values and priorities align with your organization's values and mission. This will have

a major bearing on your decision making in the areas of career management and professional development.

5 Are you a good fit for your organization? This will have a huge influence on how far your employer will take you in your professional development and career.

6 When an associate asks you about your previous bosses, do you tend to respond that you dislike all of them? If so, reflect on how you can reframe this and what you can change.

7 Assess on a scale from 1 to 10 (1 is poor; 10 is strong) your satisfaction with each of these four areas in your life: work/education, leisure, relationships, and health.

8 Evaluate if you are a leader who delivers good intentions or a leader who delivers actions. Create a list of what you wanted to do last week and what you actually did.

9 Assess your abilities in these four general areas:

- Handling conflict, contrary viewpoints, or rejection of your ideas

- Managing your ego

- Seeing and understanding situations through the eyes of others

- Frequency and degree of anger

Personal Development through Feedback and Relationships

10 Take advantage of feedback from assessments (360-degree, performance reviews, work styles) to see yourself through the eyes of others. When you receive it, don't rationalize it or be defensive.

11 Learn the competencies and criteria on which you're being evaluated. What are the measurable aspects of your job and your associated performance levels? Discuss this with your manager and team to determine development opportunities and better achieve group expectations. Identify your five strengths as well as five areas to improve.

12 Review your notes from feedback sessions and performance reviews with your bosses in recent years. What trends do you see? What no longer appears as a weakness? This is valuable data for you.

13 Solicit feedback from your people on your management style and effectiveness.

14 Share your personal development intentions with a coach or mentor, trusted colleague, or friend. They will encourage and support you, and provide incentive to stick to your goal.

Strategies for Personal Development

15 Leverage and build on your strengths while working on areas where you need improvement. It's your strengths that have gotten you this far! Keep this perspective as you move forward: don't overfocus on weaknesses.

16 As you design a plan of attack on your targeted areas, consider your current workload, your manager's agenda and expectations for you, time demands away from your job, and other relevant factors. This will bring a healthy dose of reality to your plan and minimize discouragement later.

17 Don't take on too many areas for improvement. Limit yourself to working on one to five behaviors or practices at a time.

18 Be careful of being overly ambitious. You may be more inclined to "manage up" far more than "down" or "sideways." All three directions should be balanced.

19 Track your performance against your measurable job objectives. Keep a record of your quantified achievements on an ongoing basis.

20 Identify and network with people from whom you can learn in your profession, organization, and industry. Meet them in local groups and professional organizations. Become involved with them on assignments and at dinners or social events. Cultivate these relationships as a critical asset to your professional development and career advancement.

21 Keep meaningful relationships alive. Preserve them even though associates move on to other organizations. Life presents you with unpredictable and surprising changes. Your personal network of solid relationships will likely be the strongest asset you have to help you with new challenges and opportunities.

Perspective and Actions for Personal Development

22 Think of self-development as a never-ending process. It starts with personal awareness and continues with determination to improve.

23 Take your self-development plan or efforts as seriously as you would any other part of your regular job responsibilities. Stick with it.

24 Recognize that what got you to your current position may not be the skills, knowledge, and abilities that will take you to the next level. New capabilities will be required.

25 Imagine yourself in the position of greatest potential and proceed accordingly.

26 Identify and seek out assignments that will stretch you.

27 Read, study, and learn more, to be better prepared to handle greater job responsibilities.

28 When you're trying to learn a new skill, find someone who demonstrates it well. Ask them how they do it. Learn from them. Ask for advice and counsel. They will usually share constructive ideas with you to help you grow.

29 Do what you love to do. If you're not in that role, search for it and move in that direction. You will benefit all involved.

30 Don't become overpowered or intimidated by what you don't know.

31 Avoid the temptation of responding in like manner to rude or disrespectful behavior from others. Taking the high road is always the best option.

32 Get enough sleep. Good sleep or poor sleep can greatly impact your emotional intelligence (EQ). To enhance quality sleep:

- Limit caffeine intake during the day but make a hard stop at 2 p.m.

- Minimize or eliminate blue light before bed. Cell phones, laptops, tablets, and TVs emit blue light that tricks your body into thinking it's morning.

- Try not to work in bed. The mind needs to associate the bed with sleep, not with work.

33 Be patient. Behavioral change takes time. You will not succeed all the time, every time. Often, you will not be or do what you expected. Stay with it. Think of mistakes as an integral part of learning new behaviors and techniques.

34 When you generate an undesirable result, analyze it carefully to learn what you would do differently next time. Consider recording your findings in a personal learning journal to review periodically.

35 Develop and use a healthy sense of humor. It has a huge positive effect on others and makes you more approachable. Smile more.

Personal Development for Your Team

36 Take the professional development plan for your people as seriously as you would any other part of your regular job responsibilities.

37 Give feedback frequently and appropriately to your people.

38 Review our Coaching Tips in the Coaching chapter (Dimension 11) and improve your coaching skills.

39 Frequently inquire of your people what they're studying, learning, finding interesting, and discovering, and how they are applying it to their own development, as well as the development of the team, and consider its impact on the organization.

40 Look for opportunities to study, analyze, and evaluate projects and assignments with your team and with individuals to help them learn, progress, and grow. To help them grow evenly, assess what went well and what did not.

41 When appropriate, pair up team members for a specific project or period of time for coaching, mentoring, or shared learning. Select the targeted people strategically, with a more senior person who could provide the best guidance and teaching.

42 Encourage your people to view every issue, problem, or "mistake" as an opportunity for learning, growth, and progress.

43 Sense when a colleague needs to talk. When that happens, listen with limited talking and undivided attention.

Self-Assessment

Using the scale provided, rate yourself on the following leadership behaviors.

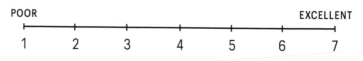

POOR   EXCELLENT

1   2   3   4   5   6   7

____ I dedicate time each week for personal development.

____ I utilize my peers and/or colleagues as coaches and feedback providers.

____ I attend professional development and networking events.

____ I strive to apply new tools or learning in my day-to-day work.

____ I balance my home and work life.

____ I maintain interests and hobbies outside of work.

____ I have good relationships inside and outside of work.

Comments

_____

_____

_____

_____

_____

_____

_____

_____

_____

_____

Action-Planning Notes

What three things in this section will help you be a better leader?

1

_____

_____

_____

2

_____

_____

_____

3

_____

_____

_____

What would change if you started or continued doing these three things?

_____

_____

_____

_____

How can you implement these changes?

_____

_____

_____

_____

Dimension 15
Team Building

"Coming together is a beginning. Keeping together is progress. Working together is success."

HENRY FORD

Do I unify my team with a common vision?
Do I clarify team roles and responsibilities?
Do I leverage the strengths and skills of team members?

What Is Team Building?

Team building is helping a group of individuals work together to accomplish a common goal. A well-orchestrated team will leverage the strengths of each member in an atmosphere of belonging and encouragement. As the team leader, you'll set the strategic direction, create the plan, and organize the members. To drive performance, you'll magnify the synergy and abilities of the team through skilled listening, communication, coaching, and training.

What it looks like:

* Clarifying roles, responsibilities, and accountability

* Encouraging healthy debate, brainstorming, and team problem solving

* Creating an environment of trust, inclusion, and open communication

* Recognizing the efforts and accomplishments of each team member

What it is not:

* Being dishonest, unethical, or using fear instead of trust
* Failing to include the team in setting direction and goals
* Ignoring team feedback to the leader
* Neglecting to address issues that affect the team

What it looks like when it is overused:

* Involving everyone on the team for every decision

* Making sure the team is happy at the expense of business results

* Focusing so much on team processes that it hinders flexibility

* Holding long, frequent meetings with the team that prevent execution

When you build teams effectively, you can drive better business and people performance. Here are some of the results you can achieve.

Business results:

- Achieving a higher-quality output with greater buy-in
- Clear roles and responsibilities for high performance
- Connecting day-to-day actions to greater purposes
- Fostering new ideas and product, service, or process innovation

People results:

- Leveraging the strengths of each person
- Fully engaging the hearts and heads of employees
- Building a culture of open communication and inclusion
- Developing and retaining employees

Coaching Tips

Being a Good Team Leader

1 Be an honest, ethical role model for your team. They will mirror your behaviors and attitudes.

2 Be seen as a facilitator for the team rather than as a "boss"— and don't try to be popular or everyone's friend. Keep a healthy balance between leader and cheerleader.

3 Be a "barrier breaker." Effective team leaders do all they can to clear the road so the team can keep moving ahead.

4 Get out among your people. Be visible. Don't isolate yourself.

5 Be approachable! Make sure you're available and easy to approach with ideas, questions, or requests for your opinion. Be interested in their concerns. Don't appear too busy to be available for your team.

6 Champion your team to upper management. Your people need to see, feel, and believe that their leader goes to bat for them.

7 Support your people when problems and challenges occur, so they know you have their backs.

8 Have a passion for excellence, set the bar high, and continually encourage and challenge your team to improve.

9 Regularly express your confidence in the team. Recognize and praise the success of others rather than your own.

10 Create a safe environment for team members in which to brainstorm, share ideas, solve problems, debate, or challenge the status quo. If you don't welcome their candid input, they won't feel comfortable exploring new ideas, which will shut down opportunities for innovation or growth. Once a decision is made, everyone needs to support it.

11 Be open to the team's feedback and advice to you, their leader.

12 Greet and acknowledge people often. Their performance will reflect your attention.

13 Ask your team members how they prefer to be managed. Then test it with observations of your own.

14 Ask a trusted associate to tell you how well you receive disappointing news. Make sure they don't perceive you as someone who tends to "shoot the messenger." Be approachable and open to unpleasant surprises.

15 Take ownership when things don't go right: "It's my fault if we fail and it's the team's reward if we succeed."

16 Encourage a healthy, professional, and uplifting sense of humor to bring a refreshing influence to your team. Avoid sarcasm and put-down humor.

Building and Leading an Effective Team

17 Track your team's evolution through the four stages of a team's growth: 1) forming, 2) storming, 3) norming, and 4) performing.

18 Bring a group of diverse individuals together. Varied backgrounds and strengths will round out the overall perspective, capability, and productivity of your team.

19 Hire for culture and a desire for achieving excellence. Teach technical skills as needed.

20 As a team, set clear expectations for such internal matters as handling conflict, celebrating successes, conducting meetings, making decisions, and prioritizing time and resources. These are separate from policies, performance objectives, and job descriptions given the team by upper management and HR.

21 Help your team understand where and how their output fits with the rest of the organization. Give them the broader view of what is happening and how they fit in the bigger picture.

22 Clearly communicate your vision for your group's mission, purpose, and focus.

23 Establish and track measurable goals and objectives for your people. Encourage them to document their own achievements as they occur.

24 Meet with each member of your new team face-to-face and learn about them. Find out what's important to them, their preferences, career highlights, and goals.

25 Make sure that everyone on your team has the correct tools, training, and support for the job you ask them to do. Give them space, authority, and resources to thrive.

26 As you develop your team and delegate tasks, be very aware of your own strengths and weaknesses. Select those who complement you. Delegate the areas or tasks to them that they'll do better than you will.

27 Give feedback frequently and appropriately to your people—positive in public, negative in private—and separate the person from the behavior.

28 Identify the individuals and teams who are meeting or surpassing their targeted metrics. Have them partner with others who are struggling, to share their best practices.

29 Show your interest in your team's progress on tasks and projects with status reports that will enable you to provide support and needed resources.

30 Encourage cross-functional collaboration by helping your people establish healthy, professional relationships with others outside the team or group.

31 Be alert for large and small accomplishments that merit recognition and celebration, within your own team and across the organization.

32 Ask tough questions. Get your people to think—and think hard.

33 When your team is not performing to the expected level, be open to and invite their feedback on root issues and how to resolve them.

34 When your people bring you their problems, listen to them, guide and support them, but don't solve the issues. Let them own the problems and solutions.

35 When you find that your team is in disagreement, clarify the "what" from the "how." Align on the "what" and leave the "how" up to the team.

36 Consider the appropriateness of "self-directed" teams that determine their own purpose, direction, and approach without an official leader. The team members share leadership. Under certain circumstances, this arrangement can be very productive and advantageous—but direction and training are needed to get them started.

Managing a Remote or Virtual Team

37 Compensate for physical distance in part by overcommunicating to create an inclusive, familiar, comfortable, trusting environment. Deliver on what you promise or explain clearly why you can't.

38 Schedule a regular (preferably weekly) thirty-minute one-on-one phone or video call with each member of your team to build trust and familiarity.

39 Where appropriate, consider weekly team check-in calls preceded by a brief emailed agenda.

40 Spend the first few minutes of your weekly or monthly team call catching up on icebreakers such as appropriate family activities or sporting events. This will add a personal touch to the overall team-building mood of the call.

41 Agree with your team members in advance about which types of decisions they will make on their own and which are too important to make alone.

42 Establish ground rules, expectations, and a process for communicating urgent, routine, and other types of messages.

43 Use video calls whenever possible to take advantage of facial expressions and other nonverbal cues while working through problem solving and decision making.

44 Make virtual meetings interactive, with questions and/or formal or informal polls, to increase engagement and help prevent multitasking.

45 Celebrate successes and make sure your remote people are included in every celebration.

46 Actively communicate and share information with each person to help everyone feel in the loop.

Self-Assessment

Using the scale provided, rate yourself on the following leadership behaviors.

POOR						EXCELLENT
1	2	3	4	5	6	7

_____ I create and promote an environment for open and honest communication.

_____ I trust my people.

_____ My people trust each other.

_____ My people trust me.

_____ I leverage the strengths of each team member.

_____ I recognize the efforts and accomplishments of each team member.

Comments

_____

_____

_____

_____

_____

_____

_____

_____

_____

_____

_____

Action-Planning Notes

What three things in this section will help you be a better leader?

1

_____

_____

_____

2

_____

_____

_____

3

_____

_____

_____

What would change if you started or continued doing these three things?

_____

_____

_____

_____

How can you implement these changes?

_____

_____

_____

_____

Dimension 16
Time Management

"Work expands so as to fill the time
available for its completion."

CYRIL NORTHCOTE PARKINSON

Do I delegate effectively?
Do I prioritize my responsibilities and tasks?
Do I run meetings efficiently?

What Is Time Management?

Time management is the ability to plan and control how you spend the hours in your day to effectively accomplish your goals and meet deadlines. Time management is at the heart of every second of every day of your life, at work and at home. How time is used determines how we live and who we become. Personal motivation and discipline, along with teachable techniques, are essential to using your time wisely. By adding these skills to your daily behaviors, you can dramatically improve how you use the valuable resource of time.

What it looks like:

- Matching time commitments to business priorities
- Being sensitive to work–life balance
- Setting aside personal catch-up time and unstructured time
- Running purposeful, efficient meetings

What it is not:

- Thinking that busy equals accomplishment

- Postponing priorities for less important matters

- Neglecting to delegate tasks

- Ignoring the face time or support needs of your people

What it looks like when it is overused:

- Unable to be spontaneous because it is different from existing plans

- Assuming that doing more of something is always the best approach

- Not valuing time to rest and recharge

- Ignoring the need for sufficient sleep

When you manage time effectively, you can drive better business and people performance. Here are some of the results you can achieve.

Business results:

- Managing competing priorities
- Consistently meeting important deadlines

- Effectively managing one's calendar and meeting schedule
- Fostering credibility with all stakeholders

People results:

- Organizing your time to develop your people
- Building a personal reputation of following through
- Effectively integrating home and work
- Delegating for better results and employee development

Coaching Tips

Managing Time Well as a Leader

1 Focus on your strategy and set your goals to support it—daily, weekly, monthly, quarterly.

2 At the start of each day, know what your most important tasks are.

3 Identify the part of the day when you're most effective and schedule mission-critical items then.

4 Have your people represent you at meetings when possible. It will give them an opportunity for growth.

5 Take full advantage of the power of deadlines. Assign them to yourself and others.

6 Recognize small bits of time as valuable gifts. Think of all the "ten-minute chunks" that you have in a day, at airports, in taxis, or waiting for others. Use them to chip away at projects or think of ways your team or organization can be more effective. You'll be surprised at your progress over time.

7 Your mind is limited in its scope, so concentrate on only a few actions or projects at a time. Otherwise you will dilute your effectiveness in all of your activities.

8 Manage your inbox by using the two-minute rule: if it will take you two minutes or less, deal with it right now: respond to the message, file it, or share it with a colleague.

9 Honor "the zone." You do your best work when your mind is in the zone. When writing an article, analyzing data, wording a critical email, creating a presentation, or reviewing a contract, avoid distractions because it takes at least fifteen minutes to reenter the zone.

10 When in charge of meetings, start and end them on time.

11 If you travel often, have a set of duplicate items, such as power chargers, cords, and toiletries, to save you time.

12 Schedule in breaks. Taking a short walk, stretching, or just moving can get the creative juices flowing again, making your work more productive. Don't fall into the trap of being "too busy" to take a short break from the task at hand. Your critical thinking abilities will be better after regular breaks.

13 Analyze the way you run meetings. Can they be shorter? Do you use an agenda? Are items brought up that could be handled offline with just one person? Ask your people for their input and ideas for overall improvements.

14 Schedule personal, private catch-up time. Many executives set aside time early each morning.

15 Hold meetings during which everyone stands—it can change the pace and often make for a shorter meeting.

16 Assign value of importance and effort to tasks: drop, delay, delegate, or do.

17 Establish a select few key priorities based largely on what's truly important to your boss and senior management. Communicate them often. Schedule your time to spend at least 30 to 50 percent on your highest priorities.

18 Help your people recognize the difference between long hours and actual results. Busy does not always translate into accomplishment. Help them identify ways they can be more efficient and productive.

19 Ask yourself and your team if you both are focusing time and resources on the highest-priority items. Less important items can be tempting because they seem easier or more appealing, but they are actually distracting from the truly critical items.

20 Minimize the number of tasks you are assigned after a meeting. Make sure you are doing only the tasks that only you in your position can do.

21 Do the hardest tasks first. You'll be pleasantly surprised by how much emotional satisfaction and progress you can achieve by just getting started.

22 Ask questions before saying yes. Clarify deadlines and details, quantify available resources, identify and agree on necessary support. Learn to say no when appropriate.

23 At the close of each week, take a time-out to personally review how you've used your time. Determine if you've made progress on key or major actions, projects, and activities that you committed to do.

24 Handle each piece of paper or electronic message only once.

25 Especially for large projects, take a first step—any step! This will decrease anxiety and enable you to better prioritize the other items on the list, and to breathe easier.

26 Before leaving work each day, briefly plan for tomorrow.

Avoiding Hindrances to Time Management

27 Don't be so controlled by your inbox, social media, or texting, especially when they distract you at inappropriate times.

28 If you consistently spend excessive time looking for things, overhaul your system.

29 Examine what is stopping you or your people from working through problems. How can they become more effective in addressing obstacles?

30 Parkinson's Law says that "work expands to fill the time available for its completion." Be aware of this typical behavioral tendency when establishing deadlines for yourself and others.

31 Don't take on other people's responsibilities. This can happen to you without even realizing it. Are you taking on any of these right now?

32 When tempted to procrastinate on a project, ask yourself, "How much tension and stress am I adding to my plate by *not* taking action? Is it worth it?"

33 Be sure you aren't guided solely by what you like and dislike.

34 Break up your problems into smaller, more manageable tasks.

Self-Assessment

Using the scale provided, rate yourself on the following leadership behaviors.

POOR   EXCELLENT

  1   2   3   4   5   6   7

____ I regularly prioritize my daily tasks and responsibilities.

____ I effectively manage short- and long-term objectives and commitments.

____ I know how to identify and stop doing non-core activities.

____ I clearly delegate activities to others.

____ I control my schedule instead of my schedule controlling me.

____ I know what to say no to.

____ I am prepared for meetings.

____ I use electronic devices to my advantage.

Comments

_____

_____

_____

_____

_____

_____

_____

_____

_____

Action-Planning Notes

What three things in this section will help you be a better leader?

1

_____

_____

_____

2

_____

_____

_____

3

_____

_____

_____

What would change if you started or continued doing these three things?

_____

_____

_____

_____

How can you implement these changes?

_____

_____

_____

_____

Dimension 17
Valuing Others

"Kind words can be short and easy to
speak, but their echoes are truly endless."

MOTHER TERESA

Do I treat others with dignity?
Do I understand their needs and concerns?
Do I recognize and celebrate successes?

What Is Valuing Others?

Valuing others is the ability to recognize people's potential and
let them know that their capabilities, experience, and contributions are important. It's celebrating employee performance
and helping others develop a strong sense of personal accomplishment. It is taking an active interest in people and listening
to their ideas. Each of us has a need to feel valued in our

sphere of influence, and this is accomplished through understanding the concerns of others and treating them with dignity.

What it looks like:

* Treating others with fairness and understanding
* Ensuring opinions are heard and respected
* Including those affected in the decision-making process
* Being available to your people

What it is not:

* Being too busy to listen to concerns and feelings
* Overlooking or ignoring the contributions of others
* Demeaning others through sarcasm, put-downs, and side comments
* Making assumptions and generalizations

What it looks like when it is overused:

* Focusing on some of the team at the expense of others
* Feeling as though you need to compliment and reinforce every action
* Overburdening the strengths of your star performers
* Treating all feedback the same on every decision

When you value others, you can drive better business and people performance. Here are some of the results you can achieve.

Business results:

* Creating an inclusive, inspiring culture
* Attracting and retaining top talent
* Establishing ownership to drive productivity
* Strengthening buy-in for change and innovation

People results:

- Achieving alignment through open communication
- Securing commitment from others
- Leveraging the strengths and expertise of the team
- Staff engagement, empowerment, and development

Coaching Tips

Fostering an Atmosphere of Valuing Others

1 Never demean people.

2 Respect the other person's time by considering their pressures and priorities.

3 Through your actions and nonverbal behaviors, demonstrate the same level of respect to everyone, at all professional levels in your organization.

4 Remember how you felt when you were younger in your career. This will remind you of the way others may feel right now. Consider their feelings, concerns, and attitudes as you make decisions.

5 Share credit often.

6 Try your best to be available when others need you.

7 Get into the habit of complimenting others, sincerely and genuinely pointing out what they do well.

8 Be motivated to help others, not yourself. Seek to make them look good. As a result, their commitment to you will be much higher.

9 Become familiar with various personality assessments (such as the Myers-Briggs Type Indicator) to give you a greater

understanding and appreciation for the many varieties of people you work with and how your style or type relates to them.

10 Illustrate to others that you value their thoughts and ideas by writing down their key points during meetings. This simple gesture will let them know you're serious and that what they're saying is important.

11 Use personal, handwritten notes expressing specific appreciation for extra-mile efforts.

12 Look for relevant developmental programs and courses and share these with others.

13 Speak out when others are not being valued or recognized for their contributions. Encourage others to share their thoughts and suggestions. Help them be heard. See that their views are considered and taken into account.

14 As difficult as it may be, show the same degree of respect to those with whom you disagree or with whom you've had unpleasant experiences.

Building Relationships

15 Call people by name. Learn what they prefer to be called and use it (nicknames, initials, shortened names). Spell their names correctly in written messages.

16 Build rapport with associates by asking questions that show genuine interest in them. Where do they live? How long have they worked here? What's their favorite vacation? What do they enjoy doing after work?

17 Go to their workstation or cubicle to get to know them. Note any personal photos and mementos they have on display

and build conversations around them. Get to know the strengths of each team member. Identify what activities and tasks energize them.

18 Pay attention to what's important to your people and listen to what they say.

19 Recognize who depends on you for counsel, suggestions, and advice. You play a key role in their professional lives. Include them in your network. Value them. Reciprocate with them. These relationships will be an asset to you and to them, now and in the future.

20 Learn about your bosses. Make the effort to find out their style, values, expectations, pet peeves, and experiences. This will help you relate to them and understand them better, which will lead to a more positive relationship with them. It will also let you know how you can respond most favorably to them and their requests.

21 Learn what your bosses are responsible for delivering to their bosses. That's the most pressing challenge they have. Look for ways to help them directly or indirectly with that objective.

22 As a first step with a new team, meet with each one, face-to-face, and learn about them. Find out what's important to them, their preferences, career highlights, and goals. Doing this sincerely, with no hidden agenda, will begin to break down barriers between them and the "new boss," allowing you to build on shared views and values.

23 Mentor others officially or unofficially. Help them learn the ropes, paths to opportunities, and steps to take for growth and recognition.

24 Recognize that the way your people view their relationship with you and your company will affect their attitude and loyalty. Of all the factors that contribute to your people's attitude, your behavior toward them is the single most important influence.

25 Brush up on listening tips, including "active listening."

26 Know when to shift between "listen to solve" and "listen to just listen."

27 Review coaching and delegating tips for ways to be more involved in your people's growth and development.

Feedback and Communication

28 Give clear, timely, specific, actionable feedback so others can realize growth opportunities and pinpoint ways to improve. Be sincere and respectful.

29 When giving corrective feedback, which can be received as negative, separate the person from the act. Discuss the behavior—reinforce the person.

30 Celebrate successes (no budget required). There are many free ways to have mini celebrations.

31 Value the contributions others make outside of work. Recognize their involvement in civic affairs, art, theater, music, athletics, church or other faith-based organizations, school, youth groups, and other volunteer work. Learn what they're involved in and acknowledge the time and talents that they contribute.

32 Develop formal awards programs that receive wide attention. Always be specific when making the presentations.

33 Be on the lookout for opportunities to publicly praise the special contributions and actions of your people—at work and in the community. Showing your admiration will ensure they feel important and valued. Be specific about where and how people have excelled.

34 Encourage members of your team to be on the lookout to praise others' contributions.

35 Build objectives into regular performance appraisals to assess and recognize positive performance. Teach supervisors how important this is in valuing others.

36 Let your people know what's happening. Keep them current on plans, directions, decisions, and concerns. Take advantage of the corporate intranet, newsletters, publications, bulletin boards, announcements, emails, and so on.

37 Let people know you understand their perspective, that you see where they're coming from and why. While you may not agree with them, you do need to demonstrate that you value their viewpoint.

38 Involve your people in decisions that affect them. They will feel valued because they know their opinions matter. They will also be far more inclined to support the final decision because they feel a sense of ownership.

39 Assess your current policies on customer appreciation and foster a customer-focused environment that proactively recognizes and acknowledges the value of your customers, your company's lifeblood.

Avoiding Devaluing Others

40 Avoid blaming. It does no good, and it damages relationships.

41 Be careful not to hurt or diminish others without realizing it through careless comments, nonverbal cues, or thoughtless behaviors that leave others feeling inferior, silly, or unqualified.

42 Before making a decision, look at the ramifications it will likely have on others. Step into their shoes. How will the end result impact them? Are there potential consequences that are unintended and harmful to others?

43 Be careful not to make assumptions and generalizations about people. These are often unfair and unkind. They also make you appear shallow and short-sighted. People deserve the right to prove themselves based on their own merits, efforts, and accomplishments.

44 Avoid interrupting people. One of the best ways to communicate that you don't value someone's input or opinion is to not allow them to finish speaking. Let them complete their thoughts. This will show them that you respect them enough to hear them out.

45 Be careful of the destructive nature of sarcasm and cutting others down. Many people engage in these behaviors, and they can be very harmful and belittling to others.

Self-Assessment

Using the scale provided, rate yourself on the following leadership behaviors.

POOR   EXCELLENT

1   2   3   4   5   6   7

____ I share credit with others.

____ I provide clear, timely, specific, and actionable feedback.

____ I try to abide by the 4:1 ratio (four positive comments to one constructive comment).

____ I am available to support my people.

____ I listen to my people's concerns and hopes.

____ I remove obstacles so my people can be successful.

____ I do not demean others through sarcasm, put-downs, or side comments.

Comments

_____

_____

_____

_____

_____

_____

_____

_____

_____

Action-Planning Notes

What three things in this section will help you be a better leader?

1
_____
_____
_____

2
_____
_____
_____

3
_____
_____
_____

What would change if you started or continued doing these three things?

_____
_____
_____
_____

How can you implement these changes?

_____
_____
_____
_____

QUADRANT IV
LEAD CHANGE

Dimension 18
Change Management

"It is not the strongest species that survive,
nor the most intelligent, but the ones
who are most responsive to change."

CHARLES DARWIN

Do you communicate a compelling vision of desired change?

Do you build organizational alliances to launch and sustain change?

Do you develop effective transition plans?

What Is Change Management?

Change management is the ability to communicate a compelling vision, lead small to large changes within an organization, and sustain the change over time. Organizations that don't respond and adapt favorably to the world around them will fail. Effective leaders study global trends to anticipate needed change. They know how to plan, implement, and communicate change, respect and manage resistance, and remain active and visible during a change effort. They successfully sponsor and support personal, team, and organizational change efforts and celebrate successes along the way.

What it looks like:

- Challenging the status quo and supporting calculated risks

- Including those affected in the change-planning process

- Assessing and optimizing the impact on internal and external customers

- Communicating the change and its outcomes to all stakeholders

What it is not:

- Assuming your change initiative is clear and logical to others

- Neglecting the potential negative realities of the effort

- Rushing the communication phase just to meet a deadline

- Minimizing the importance of the communication and sustainability plan

What it looks like when it is overused:

- Overly focusing on the changes at the expense of essential day-to-day activities

- Not recognizing when an organization has reached change saturation

* Making sure that everyone is 100 percent on board

* Spending so much time with resisters that the champions become neglected

When you manage change effectively, you can drive better business and people performance. Here are some of the results you can achieve.

Business results:

* Ensuring business agility in a global marketplace

* Innovating products and/or services to surpass the competition

* Managing and reducing risks

* Attracting new customers in new markets

People results:

* Clearly communicating the reasons and benefits of change
* Anticipating and managing employee reactions to change
* Securing buy-in from those who will implement the change
* Fostering a culture of innovation and attracting top talent

Coaching Tips

Purpose and Planning

1 Stay current on global and industry events, advances, and trends, in order to anticipate issues and implement preemptive change.

2 Decide where you are now and where you want to be. This gap will determine and define your initial change purpose and strategy.

3 Assess your business plan before moving forward: Is your plan based on catching up with your competitors or surpassing them? Will this improve your competitive advantage? Is this definitely the right move for your business?

4 Vividly paint the desired end state. Use words that will connect with those who will be impacted the most.

5 Make changes from a position of strength (proactive change), instead of from a position of defensiveness (reactive change).

6 Consider the cultural impact of the change. How will the current culture help or hinder the change?

7 When planning any type of change, include and involve those affected by it, where possible. If your team's early participation in decision making is not possible, identify alternate and/or subsequent ways you can include them in the change process.

8 Assess and project the immediate and long-term impact on your customers. Analyze and evaluate the risks to the organization and stakeholders.

9 Look at the type of change you're proposing. Is it gradual or sudden? Is there urgency? Why? These answers will help you determine your project and change communication strategies.

10 Don't avoid the toughest challenges or the hard questions. Sometimes the best options for all stakeholders are conceived from diving into the hard questions and seeking workable, forward-looking solutions.

11 Identify and define all required resources (people, technology, capital, time).

12 Explore and learn from change efforts outside your organization. Analyze what succeeded or failed when others tried similar efforts.

13 Compare your proposal to other efforts in which you've been involved. What are the differences? What went well and what didn't? How can you learn from this?

14 Plan for campaigning, lobbying, bargaining, caucusing, negotiating, collaborating, and so on, to secure essential buy-in from those affected.

Sponsors, Stakeholders, and You, the Change Leader

15 Ensure a specific sponsor exists for the change.

16 Identify, develop, and maintain internal strategic partnerships and alliances that will support the change initiative.

17 Anticipate the resistance you're likely to encounter. What are the reasons? Prepare contingencies to mitigate the resistance with these specific reasons in mind.

18 Clearly demonstrate direct benefits to employees and customers.

19 Ask employees and customers for their opinions before, during, and after the change. Seek their advice and counsel.

20 Never underestimate or overlook competing agendas.

21 Test the climate with a mentor or trusted associate. Ask them to give you an honest reality check.

22 Recognize that an important action you can take to get people to adhere to a new policy, procedure, or request is to illustrate to them how they will benefit—what's in it for them.

23 Recognize your own strengths and how they can support your change effort. Areas where you are deficient will require change partners who have the talents you lack.

24 Clearly define decision-making rights—who has the right to approve the project and who has the right to veto or kill it.

25 In many cases, as uncomfortable as it may be, be prepared to mend political fences.

26 Consider major changes you've experienced. How did you react to them? What skills did you adapt? What new talents did you develop in order to survive? In the end, did you find you could embrace new rules, new surroundings, and new people?

27 As a leader, change your day-to-day habits, meetings, questions, and reports to support the change.

28 What skills could you improve to give you the flexibility and focus to swim through any environment? Identifying and addressing them will give you greater confidence in dealing with future changes.

29 Recognize that all organizational change is ultimately personal and thus acknowledge the emotional aspects of the change for each individual.

30 Assess the team or organization's readiness for the change. Conduct a change readiness survey, interviews, or focus groups.

Implementing Change

31 Develop precise, well-researched business cases, strategies, and project and communications plans, and prepare to implement your change initiatives with confidence.

32 Be able to state the business case in two to three sentences. Frame the case for change for all levels of stakeholders.

33 Develop well-thought-out transition plans bridging the old with the new; include a communication plan, a training plan, and an implementation plan.

34 Develop a team of "believers"—the able and willing.

35 Assign a dedicated person or team to manage the change.

36 Make sure the people leading the change have the time and authority to do it.

37 Make certain that all goals, responsibilities, assignments, and schedules are crystal clear to everyone involved.

38 Establish and clearly communicate goals by which your team's performance can be monitored and measured.

39 Answer how will you address impacted processes and the continuity of work.

40 Align processes with HR systems. Do the HR systems need to change first?

41 Create a risk log. Identify low, medium, and high risks and regularly review the list. Change management is all about minimizing risks to optimize output and buy-in.

42 Revisit your communication plan. Use the right messages, at the right times, through the right media, and execute the

targeted communications for all stakeholders. Refer also to Effective Communication tips (see Dimension 2).

43 Identify clear measures of success for the project and its business impact. Report on these regularly during the change effort.

44 Once the change is underway, seek out early successes and recognize them.

45 Conduct surveys, focus groups, and so on to stay up-to-speed on concerns, impediments, frustrations, and challenges, as well as successes.

46 Recognize that the change effort may take much longer than you think.

47 Once your change has been successfully implemented, continue to view change management as a strategic tool, and create a personal plan to lead change in a proactive way that drives distinction and performance for your career, your people, and your organization!

48 Remember that sustaining the change is often more difficult than implementing it. Sunset legacy processes to avoid returning to old habits.

Self-Assessment

Using the scale provided, rate yourself on the following leadership behaviors.

POOR						EXCELLENT
1	2	3	4	5	6	7

___ I am a clear champion for change efforts.

___ I clearly communicate the business case for change to all stakeholders.

___ I use my authority to help employees remove roadblocks, which impede employees' performance and progress.

___ I have credibility in the organization.

___ I build alliances to make desired changes stick.

___ I include those affected by the change in the change process.

Comments

_____

_____

_____

_____

_____

_____

_____

_____

_____

_____

_____

_____

_____

Action-Planning Notes

What three things in this section will help you be a better leader?

1

_____

_____

_____

2

_____

_____

_____

3

_____

_____

_____

What would change if you started or continued doing these three things?

_____

_____

_____

_____

How can you implement these changes?

_____

_____

_____

_____

Dimension 19
Innovation

"Nothing is so embarrassing as watching someone
do something that you said couldn't be done."

SAM EWING

Are you open-minded?
Are you willing to take risks to further the organization?
Do you seek better ways to meet customer needs?
Do you challenge the status quo?

What Is Innovation?

Innovation is the ability to apply better and often new solutions to current or future needs. A leader's challenge is to build a culture that fosters creativity and innovation. A positive sign of such a culture is when people are excited to share and challenge ideas, and they're recognized for their contributions.

This requires a sense of openness, accountability, and trust. Ideas may come from unexpected sources, so the innovative leader is alert for them and encourages original thinking in the team and organization.

What it looks like:

- Breaking out of previous constraints

- Encouraging and rewarding new ideas or approaches

- Understanding the real needs and addressing the gaps

- Seeing mistakes and failures as opportunities to improve and learn

What it is not:

- Starting from scratch every time

- Thinking, "This is what we have always done"

- Making immediate negative judgments of new ideas

- Dismissing the unlikely or "the impossible"

What it looks like when it is overused:

- Not sticking with something long enough to learn its value

- Starting too many things at once and spreading energy and attention too thin

- Neglecting appropriate reality checks

- Getting too easily sidetracked by another shiny object or cool idea

Through innovation, you can drive better business and people performance. Here are some of the results you can achieve.

Business results:

- Providing better solutions for customers
- Encouraging healthy risk-taking
- Improving the impact of business planning
- Winning new business in new markets

People results:

- Promoting internal cooperation instead of competition
- Building a culture to question the status quo
- Encouraging and respecting diversity of thought and action
- Fostering a fun, exciting environment for productive brainstorming

Coaching Tips

Avoiding Innovation Killers

1 How you view a situation or problem usually determines how you approach it. Alter your vantage point and notice how your approach will adjust accordingly.

2 One of the biggest obstacles to innovative thinking is believing that you're not creative. Change your view of yourself—because you're much more creative than you think.

3 Don't believe that ideas are scarce and you must always compete for them at the expense of others.

4 Avoid the mindset that you have to "reinvent the wheel." You can innovate by building on the work of others. Learn from their work. Leverage it. Develop it. Try new patterns

and develop them. Create your new designs and solutions as you springboard off the thinking of others.

5 When trying something new, don't be afraid to fail or to make changes along the way. Sometimes a proposed solution works the first time; sometimes it works the hundredth time.

6 Be careful of prematurely censoring ideas or solutions. Analyze the criteria you're using. They may be too narrow or limiting.

7 Beware of idea killers:

- We've always done it this way.
- But I didn't think of it.
- The boss wouldn't like it.
- We could never afford it.
- We tried it before and it didn't work.
- It won't work.
- That's ridiculous.
- Are you crazy?

Encouraging Innovation

8 Leverage the synergy, the energy, and the spark of new ideas that can be created when differing, multigenerational minds converge to solve a problem together. This will also bring unity and buy-in to your team.

9 Draw or illustrate a problem to stimulate mental processes more than using just words. Use a large board and write out your thoughts. Keep your ideas visible for others to see.

10 Pursue outside resources to obtain a fresh perspective, such as nearby university faculty, industry representatives, and

retired colleagues, as well as trade shows, conferences, lectures, online talks/tutorials/posts, journals, and books.

11 Are you aware that six minutes of healthy, uninhibited brainstorming can often produce forty-eight ideas? Then after twenty minutes of hard evaluation, these forty-eight can be reduced to two to three solid ideas.

12 Share the concept with someone from another discipline. They will take a fresh, objective viewpoint that you probably haven't considered.

13 Blend partial answers from divergent ideas.

14 Try to resolve a problem by looking at it from different perspectives. Consider how the other stakeholders would view it. Look at it from the viewpoint of customers, vendors, your boss and boss's boss, your team, internal customers, and other associates you can identify.

15 Imagine your ideas as reality—what would change?

16 Act as if there is no risk. How will these actions open up new ideas?

17 Recall several changes of the past in which you participated. Remember that the initial reaction to them was often negative but once implemented, the changes actually proved successful, and people began getting on board and even supporting them. Be patient as others initially resist an innovative idea you're promoting.

18 Ask yourself what you could accomplish if you weren't fearful it might fail.

19 When the heat is on, turn it into a source of positive energy and an opportunity to adapt to challenges and changes with new and better ideas.

20 Try listening to music to open new mental avenues.

21 Does your organization have a process in place for rewarding great new ideas? If not, why not?

22 Acknowledge that people have higher creative periods during certain parts of the day than others. Mornings are often better than afternoons for idea generation. Take advantage of peak times.

23 Ask yourself how a nine-year-old would approach it. Or ask a nine-year-old!

Characteristics of an Innovative Leader, Team, or Organization

24 Allow time for collaboration within teams both inside and outside your department. Sometimes all it takes is to tweak a solution that was used elsewhere to fix a completely different issue.

25 Seek out and be open to the ideas of the newer or less experienced members of the team, who have a fresh perspective and can deliver ideas that are different from those of seasoned players.

26 Laughter and fun are powerful ways to make everyone more comfortable, unlock greater creativity, and generate many ideas.

27 See what those outside of your organization have done with similar issues or opportunities. What can you learn from their experience, progress, or limitations?

28 What are the competitive advantages your biggest rivals use to give them benefits over you? Analyze why they have those advantages. How can you benefit from them?

29 Review the top goals or objectives of your organization, group, and team. Look for the largest gaps in performance and identify how the organization's strengths could be used to address these gaps.

30 Decrease stress in your team. A burned-out team rarely creates positive, innovative ideas.

31 Don't focus on just catching up with your competitors. Instead, focus on surpassing them. Avoid limiting your sights, targets, and goals.

32 Have your direct reports share their business strategies and ideas with you and your peers. This will spark new ideas while enabling you to understand their alignment with the overall strategy.

33 Identify current unwritten and accepted rules that govern your organization. Notice the unspoken barriers and limitations that restrict new ideas. Rearrange the rules to allow freedom for the breakthroughs of innovation.

34 As you delegate, challenge your people to think of and try new approaches. Remind them that there's usually more than one method to accomplish assigned tasks.

35 Encourage your people to take calculated risks when appropriate.

36 Look critically at your value chain processes for ways to improve efficiencies and eliminate wasted steps. Meet with your suppliers and other business partners to assess the overall value chain flow to identify mutual actions that can benefit all of you.

37 Invite ideas, inputs, criticisms, and suggestions from employees on how your organization's strategies and processes

can be improved. Don't rely on the old suggestion box. Instead, hold skip-level meetings with various groups of employees or have brown-bag lunches to seek and encourage their ideas.

38 Don't limit the exposure of your strategic ideas to a selected few. Communicate them widely to your workforce so they feel a part of the initiative and are able to build on your ideas.

39 Keep your focus on your organization's core competencies as the foundation of your strategic vision and focus.

40 While you're launching that new product or service, implementing that new process that cuts costs or risks, or onboarding your new, top talent, never get complacent and never stop looking for the next great idea.

Self-Assessment

Using the scale provided, rate yourself on the following leadership behaviors.

POOR   EXCELLENT

1   2   3   4   5   6   7

___ I recognize that I don't have a monopoly on new ideas.

___ I welcome new ideas or approaches.

___ I encourage brainstorming without critique.

___ I am willing to take appropriate risks.

___ I am up-to-date on best practices and industry trends.

___ I am never satisfied with the status quo and try to look for new ways to make it better.

Comments

_____

_____

_____

_____

_____

_____

_____

_____

_____

_____

_____

_____

Action-Planning Notes

What three things in this section will help you be a better leader?

1

_____
_____
_____

2

_____
_____
_____

3

_____
_____
_____

What would change if you started or continued doing these three things?

_____
_____
_____

How can you implement these changes?

_____
_____
_____

Dimension 20
Inspiring Commitment

"I think when people say they dread going into
work on Monday morning, it's because they know
they are leaving a piece of themselves at home.
Why not see what happens when you challenge your
employees to bring all of their talents to their job and
reward them not for doing it just like everyone else,
but for pushing the envelope, being adventurous,
creative, and open-minded, and trying new things?"

TONY HSIEH

Do I help others feel connected to our organization?

Do I create a motivating environment?

Am I loyal to my people, my organization, and to my personal values?

What Is Inspiring Commitment?

Inspiring commitment is the ability to influence and motivate your people to higher levels of engagement and performance by earning their hearts. This requires a constant flow of communication that helps others feel energized, connected, and devoted to the organization's purpose and future. It involves an awareness of each individual's concerns, strengths, and influencers. It's understanding the importance of mutual loyalty and how to leverage the motivating factors that drive each individual's performance. Commitment starts with you, the leader, and it applies to all of your critical workplace relationships.

What it looks like:

* Placing organizational goals above personal goals

* Going beyond normal expectations

* Creating a clear vision and communicating it consistently

* Building a working environment that motivates high performance

What it is not:

* Lacking vision, drive, and clarity of purpose
* Positioning your needs and status above others
* Demonstrating unfair treatment and playing favorites
* Conveying a lack of trust by micromanaging

What it looks like when it is overused:

* Focusing so much on the future and lofty goals, the day-to-day work suffers

* Not checking in and guiding your team enough because you assume they always have it handled

* Not taking quick enough action on mediocre or poor performance to avoid negatively impacting the team or upsetting people

* Always asking what your team thinks or trying to make everyone happy before moving forward

When you inspire commitment, you can drive better business and people performance. Here are some of the results you can achieve.

Business results:

* Creating and carrying out a clear, compelling vision for excellence

* Improving customer satisfaction through employee engagement

* Achieving strategic business priorities

* Innovation in products, services, processes, and strategies

People results:

* Fostering an environment of trust, not fear
* Translating the organization's purpose for the day to day
* Building employee initiative
* Retaining top talent

Coaching Tips

Strategies for Inspiring Commitment

1 Be a champion of your team to upper management. Share the team's achievements and performance with others in a positive way to bring light and support to your people. This will clearly demonstrate your pride in them!

2 Create a vision, communicate it clearly, and rally your team around it. Be able to explain your vision in just a few sentences. Be consistent about sharing and describing the same vision. This helps create alignment with the vision.

3 Clearly define, communicate, and document performance expectations. Provide the context of how your people's work and goals fit into the larger organization. They'll perform better when they know what's expected of them—and why.

4 Let your people know how much you value their feedback on how you can improve in your job. This will give you a new perspective on what you're doing well and what you can improve on, while building your relationships with them.

5 Invite the knowledge and thoughts of those in other parts and levels of the organization—not just your own team. They will feel valued for being included, and present differing perspectives based on their unique experiences.

6 Notice how many times in a given day you ask your employees for their opinion and input. This act alone can do much to earn their hearts. They will feel included, needed, and important.

7 Be seen. Be among your people. Be visible. Don't isolate yourself.

8 Share how your core values align with the organization's core values.

9 Take a clear stand on critical issues to set priorities and provide direction.

10 Make certain your actions communicate your solid support of your people. When people sense that you have their

best interests at heart, they respond more favorably to your requests.

11 Seek ways to expand your people's influence and impact as they progress and grow. This will show you care about them and want to help them move ahead.

12 Provide your people with needed training. Learning from experience alone may not be enough to enable them to grow and develop. Sense the balance of on-the-job and more formal training, coaching, or mentoring they need to enhance their growth and progress.

13 Don't ask others to do what you are not willing to do yourself.

14 Ask your people how they're doing, and how you can help remove obstacles.

15 Seek opinions and suggestions from your people in areas that they know well.

16 Genuinely listen to your employees; this will do more to gain their commitment than any other single behavior. (See Dimension 13: Listening.)

17 Encourage your team members to get to know each other's styles, work preferences, and interests outside of work.

18 Be optimistic about the future. Resist cynical comments about the organization.

19 Inspire your people to do their best by demonstrating high performance in your own work.

20 Never underestimate the importance of interpersonal relationships and emotional intelligence (EQ). IQ is what gets you to the table. EQ is what keeps you there.

21 Take the high road by admitting when you're wrong and not blaming others or past events.

Building Relationships to Inspire Commitment

22 Encourage and promote an atmosphere of collaboration across your team and organization. Employees typically stay at a place where they feel included.

23 Know which rewards and recognitions are meaningful to each of your people. Provide these when appropriate.

24 When mentoring or coaching others, tie the feedback you give them to their performance goals.

25 Encourage and challenge your people to develop new attitudes toward risk. This can apply to current options, future prospects, and stretch assignments. Help them see that their willingness to try something will often lead to unexpected opportunities.

26 Recognize that a person's name is very important to them and use it often. When you first meet someone, try to use their name two or three times during that initial conversation. Doing so increases the likelihood you'll recall it for the next meeting.

27 Actively listen to each person with whom you're working. Let them see you're focusing on them as they speak. Put away electronics as you listen. Jot down their key points and concerns so they know you care about what they're saying.

28 Express your requests to others in ways that appeal to them—not to you.

29 Avoid perceived favoritism.

Practical Methods of Inspiring Commitment

30 Discuss expectations and priorities openly with employees and encourage their questions and input to increase their buy-in and performance.

31 Ask how individuals want to be recognized. Each person may prefer a different approach.

32 Share the "why" behind decisions and assignments whenever possible. Knowing why they are doing something will give your people a greater understanding and sense of purpose.

33 Celebrate successes—whether they are behaviors, activities, or achievements. You can do this in a variety of ways that won't cost much.

34 Let people do their jobs. Give them the space they need to complete the tasks for which they're responsible.

35 When delegating, clarify the "what" (purpose) and leave the "how" (methods) up to your employees. This will give them an increased sense of ownership.

36 Look for, recognize, and praise special contributions and actions of your associates. Be alert for things they do within the work environment and even outside work, such as service in the community, church/faith-based organizations, schools, and sports.

37 Be alert for opportunities—usually sudden and unexpected—to help colleagues who are in need.

38 Learn from your associates how they personally define empowerment. Discussing this with them will open the door to better communication while you learn what's important to them.

39 Recognize that not everyone is happy in every situation. There comes a time when some individuals will find greater satisfaction in other work areas or assignments. Accept this as OK. When it happens, help them find more suitable work in other teams or organizations. You will both be happier.

40 Willingly express gratitude. This will go a long way with those you manage.

41 Recognize that people will care more about what you need or want them to do once they know you genuinely care about them.

Avoiding Hindrances to Inspiring Commitment

42 Be careful of the destructive nature of sarcasm and cutting others down. Many people engage in these behaviors, and they can be very harmful and belittling to others.

43 Don't seek or claim credit when it's not deserved.

44 Don't rotate bald tires. In other words, don't promote or transfer someone who is not doing a good job.

45 If your people bring you their problems, don't solve them. Give them guidance and support, but let them own their problems and the solutions.

46 Don't try to be popular or everyone's friend. You need to function at a different level and maintain professional perspective for the benefit of the overall team and the organization.

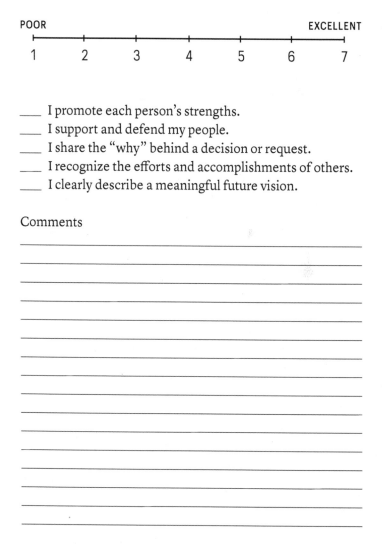

Self-Assessment

Using the scale provided, rate yourself on the following leadership behaviors.

POOR   EXCELLENT

| 1 | 2 | 3 | 4 | 5 | 6 | 7 |

___ I promote each person's strengths.

___ I support and defend my people.

___ I share the "why" behind a decision or request.

___ I recognize the efforts and accomplishments of others.

___ I clearly describe a meaningful future vision.

Comments

_____

_____

_____

_____

_____

_____

_____

_____

_____

_____

_____

_____

_____

_____

_____

Action-Planning Notes

What three things in this section will help you be a better leader?

1

_____

_____

_____

2

_____

_____

_____

3

_____

_____

_____

What would change if you started or continued doing these three things?

_____

_____

_____

_____

How can you implement these changes?

_____

_____

_____

_____

Dimension 21
Organizational Savvy

"Organizational savvy is having the necessary information
and internal knowledge of people, systems, cultures,
and politics to influence others to *get things done.*"

ANONYMOUS

Do you leverage the unofficial organizational chart to
get things done?

Do you create partnerships to benefit performance?

Do you build, maintain, and learn from your external
network?

What Is Organizational Savvy?
Organizational savvy is knowing how to get things done
through formal and informal channels, and understanding the

cultural dynamics of the organization. It's knowing who knows whom, who can do what, who's willing, who has the authority, who can make it happen, who knows the history, who knows the unwritten rules, who can break the logjam, who knows the way around policies, who owes you a favor, and who likes a good challenge. It's all about the connections you build, how you influence others, and your agility in leveraging these relationships, in ethical ways, to get what needs to be done, *done*.

What it looks like:

- Learning the backgrounds and styles of key players

- Grasping the organizational systems, subsystems, and processes

- Establishing a network of trusting relationships

- Understanding timing and politically sensitive topics

What it is not:

- Always saying yes to senior management
- Being insincere or self-serving
- Believing others should always come to you
- Ignoring the political aspects of your organization

What it looks like when it is overused:

- Getting caught up in political games and forgetting your core values

- Supporting unethical or immoral activities to go along with others

- Ignoring your own interests while only pursuing the self-serving interests of others

- Treating other people like objects instead of like people

With organizational savvy, you can drive better business and people performance. Here are some of the results you can achieve.

Business results:

* Securing the resources to accomplish priorities
* Gaining new ideas and approaches to drive improvements
* Honoring the past while forging a new future
* Leveraging information to stay ahead of the competition

People results:

* Building strategic relationships and partnerships
* Navigating the political landscape
* Influencing key decision makers to effect change
* Fostering team collaboration and development

Coaching Tips

Building Organizational Savvy

1 Know the official organizational chart—and the unofficial one. Know boundaries and crossovers of functional responsibilities. Be knowledgeable about the unofficial and official key players in the organization, their personalities, philosophies, behaviors, attitudes, track records, and agendas. Know who has "real" power.

2 Pay close attention to what's happening in the work environment: from a 500-foot point of view and a 50,000-foot point of view.

3 Know the names, faces, history, and goals of your organization's major customers and suppliers.

4 Stay current on best practices, industry, and socioeconomic trends.

5 Be aware of your major competitors and their methods—external *and* internal.

6 Influence where you have no authority by building your personal credibility.

7 Analyze and decide what leadership style your department or organization needs now and in the future, and learn how to best provide that style.

8 Learn how you're viewed in the company from the perspective of your boss or other senior colleagues and modify your behavior accordingly.

9 Pay attention to the grapevine as a potent source of information. Just don't believe—or repeat—everything you hear.

10 Do consistently good work and strategically make it visible to key decision makers.

11 When you anticipate resistance to an idea you're preparing to present to a key group, pre-sell it to members of the group one at a time (lobbying).

12 Don't assume that a meeting is apolitical. In other words, be aware of existing concerns and hopes from key influencers.

13 When significant events happen in your company, learn how they happened, who drove them, why they happened, and the special or unusual circumstances.

14 Recognize that influence is often determined by the strength of your bonds with your associates. These trusting relationships are built on common goals, shared values, and commitment to overall objectives.

15 Always be open to bad, disappointing, or contrary news. This will keep you from becoming isolated. Demonstrate to others how you eagerly seek information from them so you're never caught out of the loop or unaware. Don't shoot the messenger.

16 Recognize that the higher you move in the organization, the more you must wear at least two hats: with your own team and with the senior team of your peers. Some leaders fail because they're able to wear only one hat, with their own team. They can't seem to remove it when necessary and replace it with the broader-focused hat requiring them to see issues from a grander scale.

17 As a leader, consider the many you rely on to accomplish your tasks and meet your goals. Do you acknowledge and recognize their contributions? What do you provide them in return? You steadfastly and openly support your boss and the organization above you. Neither you nor the team you lead can be successful otherwise.

18 Help your team understand where and how their output fits with the rest of the organization. Help them establish healthy, professional relationships with others outside of their own function and team or department. These relationships can open the door to collaboration, opportunity, and innovation within the company.

19 Be forward-thinking. Focus on developing solutions and not dwelling on problems.

Gaining Organizational Savvy

20 Learn internal "partnerships" and unofficial strong relationships between key individuals so you can leverage and capitalize on them.

21 Learn who knows whom outside of work. What are the relationships?

22 Identify the opinion leaders and the networkers in organizations.

23 Learn characteristics and attitudes of key decision makers to help develop your team's strategies when you need senior management's support. Know their stand on relevant issues (pros, cons, neutral) to help ensure the success of your plan.

24 Establish a network of professionals within your organization who know the business, the company, the products, the services, the customers, and the markets—especially those who affect your own sphere of concern and interest. Rotate through the list regularly for a lunch or brief visit to learn their perspective and opinions. Get to know them. Allow them to know you.

25 What "givebacks" can you offer the people with whom you network? Don't neglect to ask, "How can I help you?"

26 Attend social gatherings and events in your organization. Meet people from various levels and responsibilities. Recognize them later in hallways or other places. Call them by name. Stay in touch. You and your associates will find mutual value in these relationships as a source of information and support.

27 Develop external professional relationships with people who have similar job titles or assignments. Meet with some of them informally to share concerns and challenges. Discreetly sharing selected job issues may prove helpful to you and them. They may have answers, techniques, and solutions that you'll want to consider in solving some of the challenges you're facing, and vice versa.

28 Identify reports and metrics that your influences consider important. Stay current of the trends and concerns in this data.

29 Learn the history of critical parts of the company and culture that affect your group—what has worked, what hasn't worked, and why.

30 Analyze which systems, processes, behaviors, and patterns best suit the needs of the overall organization. Which ones should be adopted and implemented across the entire enterprise?

31 Replace internal competition with encouraging and mutually beneficial cooperation. Your primary competition should be directed at your organization's industry rivals.

32 Ask your boss and other members of senior management how they define success, what it looks like, what it does *not* look like, and what advice they have for you. This will open your eyes to a new level of expectations and viewpoints that will help you direct your own team.

33 There's much-needed information out there that your direct reports may not be sharing in your staff meeting. Go find it! Mingle!

34 A handy rule of thumb is the word SEEK:

- Support—who can provide it for you

- Equipment—what you'll need and how to get it

- Experience—who knows the right people and their respective "hot buttons"

- Knowledge—who knows how things really work and how things get done

Avoiding Hindrances to Organizational Savvy

35 Avoid the statement or feeling of "It's not my job!"

36 Do you like to be different in the way you dress, your appearance, style, and behavior? If so, you'll face a challenge in fitting in with the culture of your company. Anticipate the likely results of your choices and consciously decide if the risk to your career is worth it. There are many appropriate ways to establish your own identity and be true to your values.

37 Avoid the attitude of seeing senior management as your adversary. Others will pick up on this quickly.

38 Remain open to help from others—internal and external to your organization. This help may come in the form of a new idea, a sounding board, confirmation of a strategic direction, or a hundred other different ways. Don't close yourself off from this source of power and learning.

39 Avoid being myopic and focusing only on your own team. Focus your view of your organization up, down, and side to side. All of these perspectives are essential for you to see the big picture, which includes goals, positions, and people. Broaden your perspective and your view of what's really happening, and what's important to your associates.

40 Don't allow differences of hierarchy and position to inhibit trusting relationships. Establish trusting relationships at all levels.

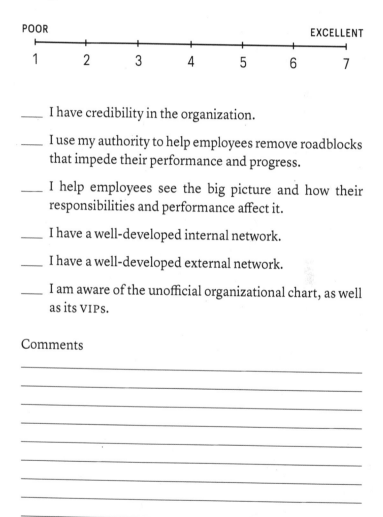

Self-Assessment

Using the scale provided, rate yourself on the following leadership behaviors.

POOR   EXCELLENT

1   2   3   4   5   6   7

____ I have credibility in the organization.

____ I use my authority to help employees remove roadblocks that impede their performance and progress.

____ I help employees see the big picture and how their responsibilities and performance affect it.

____ I have a well-developed internal network.

____ I have a well-developed external network.

____ I am aware of the unofficial organizational chart, as well as its VIPs.

Comments

_____

_____

_____

_____

_____

_____

_____

_____

_____

_____

Action-Planning Notes

What three things in this section will help you be a better leader?

1

_____
_____
_____

2

_____
_____
_____

3

_____
_____
_____

What would change if you started or continued doing these three things?

_____
_____
_____
_____

How can you implement these changes?

_____
_____
_____
_____

PART III

ASSESSING AND PLANNING

Taking the LEAD NOW!
Assessments

SSESSING YOUR leadership ability is an essential step in identifying where to focus your development efforts. As you dive into the LEAD NOW! Model, we have three ways for you to assess how well you do in each Leadership Dimension. Select which approach makes sense for you and allow the assessment process to help define your action plan.

1 **LEAD NOW! Self-Study Assessment** Use the short self-assessment at the end of each Leadership Dimension chapter, and then use the Self-Study Quadrant Assessment below.

2 **LEAD NOW! Self-Assessment** Use the assessment through Stewart Leadership (stewartleadership.com/solutions/assessments) to measure both leadership effectiveness (what you are good at) and preference (what you like to do).

3 **LEAD NOW! 360 Assessment** Use the online assessment through Stewart Leadership (stewartleadership.com/solutions/assessments) to measure your leadership

effectiveness through the perceptions of your boss, direct reports, peers, customers, and yourself.

1. LEAD NOW! Self-Study Quadrant Assessment

Now that you've completed the self-assessment at the end of each of the Dimensions, consider your personal leadership development in each of the four quadrants of the LEAD NOW! Model. Refer to the model on page 259 and rate your understanding and skill in each quadrant using the following scale.

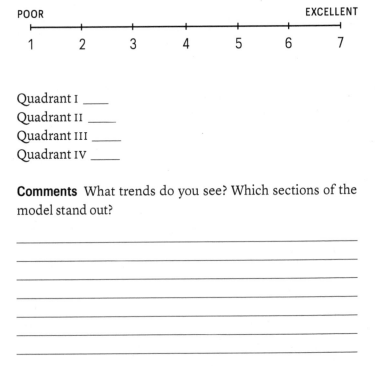

POOR   EXCELLENT

1   2   3   4   5   6   7

Quadrant I _____
Quadrant II _____
Quadrant III _____
Quadrant IV _____

Comments What trends do you see? Which sections of the model stand out?

_____

_____

_____

_____

_____

_____

_____

As you briefly review the Leadership Dimensions, complete an initial quick self-assessment. Use the following scale to "evaluate" your mastery of each Dimension.

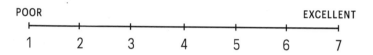

POOR   EXCELLENT

1   2   3   4   5   6   7

Quadrant I: Create Purpose
- Customer Focus _____
- Effective Communication _____
- Presentation Skills _____
- Strategic Thinking _____

Quadrant II: Deliver Excellence
- Decision Making _____
- Delegating _____
- Dependability _____
- Focusing on Results _____
- Personal Integrity _____
- Problem Solving _____

Quadrant III: Develop Self & Others
- Coaching _____
- Ego Management _____
- Listening _____
- Personal Development _____
- Team Building _____
- Time Management _____
- Valuing Others _____

Quadrant IV: Lead Change
* Change Management _____
* Innovation _____
* Inspiring Commitment _____
* Organizational Savvy _____

Comments What trends do you see? Which Dimensions in the model stand out? Your highest-rated Dimensions represent strengths you should leverage, while your lowest-rated could be improved.

_____

_____

_____

_____

_____

_____

Reflection
It is common for leaders to feel comfortable in one area and not in another. For example, some may excel in developing business strategy and yet struggle in adjusting their leadership style in developing others. Other leaders may feel more comfortable championing a change effort, but have difficulty defining a process.

This assessment will become your "baseline"—the starting point for measurable growth and sustainable change in your leadership behaviors.

Leadership Goal Worksheet
At the end of this book, we have included action plan templates to help you make a plan for improved leadership. As

a preparation for formalizing those action plans, we have included the following questions to help you identify why you need to improve, your desire to change, and your initial thoughts regarding how and/or what to change:

- What do I need to develop, improve, or change?

- Why do I feel the need to change this? What could be the cause of this need?

- How will I make this a priority?

LEAD NOW! Model Description

Quadrant I: Create Purpose (Externally Focused Business Results)

As a leader, you are responsible for defining the group's vision and strategy. Creating purpose identifies what the organization stands for, what it is going to do, and how it is positioned in the marketplace. This involves studying the competition, thoroughly knowing the customer, analyzing industry trends, setting strategy, and communicating effectively to others.

Quadrant II: Deliver Excellence (Internally Focused Business Results)

As a leader, you are responsible for delivering operational excellence—translating the strategy into day-to-day execution for the organization. This involves clear decision making, the ability to build consistent and measurable processes, continuous improvement, and behaving with integrity.

Quadrant III: Develop Self & Others (Internally Focused People Results)

As a leader, you must value learning for yourself and for others. This involves seeking personal improvement opportunities, building and managing team dynamics, honing technical expertise, managing one's time, coaching and developing others, and managing one's ego.

Quadrant IV: Lead Change (Externally Focused People Results)

As a leader, you are responsible for creating and championing change efforts that will benefit the organization. This involves influencing key decision makers, sponsoring change projects, empowering stakeholders, encouraging innovation, managing resistance, and making change stick.

2. LEAD NOW! Self-Assessment

The LEAD NOW! Self-Assessment will provide you with critical information on how your leadership effectiveness aligns with your leadership preferences (what you like to do) and how you can build your leadership ability. This is a powerful way of identifying how your strengths (what energizes you) are being leveraged—or not—as a leader.

This assessment is ideal for

* Individuals wanting personal improvement in their current leadership role

* Individuals preparing for or transitioning into a management or leadership position

* Leadership teams wanting to secure the right "fit" for individuals

Features

* Assessment type: Behavioral leadership assessment

* Time to complete: fifteen to twenty minutes

* Format: Online survey of forty-five questions and five short responses

* Results at three levels of analysis: four quadrants, twenty-one Dimensions, and forty-five behaviors

* Personalized report detailing immediate next steps

Please visit stewartleadership.com to learn more about this assessment and how to purchase this tool for you and your leaders.

How important is it to understand how your effectiveness relates to what you like to do? Consider the following two leaders, who have two very different stories.

When I was younger, I heard about an aerospace executive who detested his job. He had been doing the same job for years, and he hated it. This became very evident when you asked him about work. He could be in the middle of talking about any other topic—sports, family, the weather—but once someone asked him about work, his entire countenance soured; he became distant and guarded, and the conversation suddenly became much less pleasant. While he probably did his job just fine, there was definitely no love for it any longer.

In contrast, consider an executive I was recently coaching. She had just been given another team, which doubled her scope and responsibility. This new team was in a new functional area for her. She was excited! She recognized that her skills were going to be stretched and her effectiveness challenged. She liked the learning curve ahead of her, especially as she could improve her ability to coach her team, manage her calendar better, and set clear direction for the disparate groups under her responsibility.

These tales of two very different executives illustrate two common scenarios leaders find themselves in.

The first scenario is when someone's preference for the job is significantly less than their ability to effectively perform their job. They may have the technical competence to do it, but they no longer have the passion or engagement for it. This is called "misaligned energy," and it leads to people not showing up and offering their best selves in helping their team and the organization.

This can be a very challenging situation because the individual has usually displayed operational excellence in the past, but is now no longer challenged or feeling supported. Their energy—where they get their strength—is absent from their job. The solution for this scenario is candid conversation and introspection. The person is not being served well, nor are they serving the organization well. If nothing changes, their disengagement may grow and negatively impact the team.

The second scenario occurs when someone's interest in doing the job is greater than their ability to complete it. In other words, they may not have all of the skills to be highly effective, but they sure want to be. This situation is called "potential to develop." The leader's energy is focused on improving and gaining new skills, trying new approaches, and considering new ideas. They are eager and hungry to learn. The solution for this scenario is for targeted development and support. This is the ideal situation for training, mentoring, and on-the-job training.

Regardless of which situation you or one of your leaders might be in, it is important to look at how your effectiveness relates to your preference for doing the job. Understanding how those two critical variables align or not will enable you to find the right fit and development to optimize your leadership contributions to your team and organization while being honest with yourself.

How can you discover and align your preferences and your effectiveness? Our industry-leading LEAD NOW! Self-Assessment helps leaders at all levels be more effective and happier in their work.

3. LEAD NOW! 360 Assessment

The LEAD NOW! 360 Assessment enables leaders to accurately and quickly learn how their direct reports, bosses, peers, and other associates assess their leadership behaviors. This is one of the few validated 360 assessment tools on the market and has been continually improved over its several decades of being used with thousands of leaders from across the globe.

This assessment is ideal for

- Leaders transitioning into new opportunities

- Companies desiring to create a culture of development and progress

- Organizations seeking to identify high-potential employees

- Groups who are restructuring and need to create a common leadership culture

- Professionals seeking clear and tailored personal leadership growth

Features

- Assessment type: Behavioral leadership assessment

- Time to complete: thirty to forty minutes

- Format: Online survey of eighty questions and four short responses

- Results at three levels of analysis: four quadrants, twenty-one Dimensions, and eighty behaviors

- Personalized action plans based on results

- Verbatim responses

How the 360 Assessment Works

Our 360 assessments enable leaders to accurately and quickly learn how their bosses, direct reports, peers, and other associates perceive their leadership effectiveness, and provide valuable input on how they can develop themselves.

Once the 360 assessment has been completed, participants receive a comprehensive, personalized report of results that details leadership strengths, challenges, and insights that can be turned into action for immediate application.

As we talk to leaders about the power of 360 assessments, we are amazed by how energized they become. It is as if they are starving for information about their own leadership performance. Then we learn the truth—they *are* starving for information about their own leadership performance. They want to develop themselves and their teams with the goal of a world-class organization, but they lack the real and timely feedback to build and utilize their human capital and leadership abilities. This is especially true in high-growth or transforming organizations.

Six Benefits of a 360 Assessment for Leaders

1 **It sends a message that development is important.** When a leader pays attention to something, that tells others they should pay attention to it as well. When a leader focuses on personal leadership development, then their people will know this is valued in the organization. When a leader takes the time to implement and act on the insights from a 360 assessment, either using executive coaching or during a leadership program, their employees will see that leadership development is valued.

2 **It increases self-awareness and self-improvement.** We all have blind spots that might prevent us from being fully

aware of how others perceive us. We are aware of our own intentions, but the impact of our actions may create a very different story. It is through feedback from others that we increase our self-awareness of our blind spots and how our intentions may or may not show up in effective ways. Each of our four critical relationships (boss, direct reports, peers, and customers) might view our leadership effectiveness differently. Learning these perceptions can arm us with valuable information to improve our leadership intelligence.

3 **It can be applied right away, on the job.** Because a 360 assessment focuses on observable leadership behaviors, the feedback data can be immediately applied on the job. For example, if a manager scores low on the statement, "Effectively seeks multiple perspectives in solving problems," that manager knows exactly where to focus to improve their performance. The report easily gathers feedback from many evaluators, often seven to fifteen-plus people, through a twenty-minute online assessment tool. Thus, the 360 report represents hours of feedback from many key stakeholders condensed into one summary tool.

4 **It ensures data-driven action with accountability.** 360 assessments focus on specific leadership behaviors that matter to the organization. During a coaching debrief, the leader can use clear and concise 360 data to identify development trends and select one to three personal focus areas that can become the basis for an action plan. An Individual Action Plan (IAP) is approved by one's boss and targets the most important leadership development areas for each leader. During subsequent coaching sessions and also conversations with one's boss, the action plan is reviewed, updated, and tracked to ensure progress occurs.

5 **It creates a personal development conversation.** People are often well intentioned and want to help others improve, but they may not have the language or skills to have that kind of a conversation. A 360 assessment provides a clear leadership framework to form the agenda for an effective development conversation. It creates a common leadership language for a boss and manager, so they know what to focus on during a development conversation.

6 **It identifies the talent needs in your organization.** Organizations would love to know what their leaders are good at and where they need improvement. While the individual 360 report is confidential, looking at the trends across many different reports can be eye-opening. After a group of leaders participate in a 360 assessment, their scores can be amalgamated to reveal the overall strengths and challenges of the organization's leaders. Using this group data, specific leadership development experiences and programs can be created to address broader gaps. Talent reviews and succession planning are more informed through group data from 360 reports.

360 Assessments for Leadership Performance

The bottom line is that leaders need to be increasingly aware of how they perform in achieving business and people results. The 360 assessments provide specific leadership competencies and behaviors that reveal invaluable personalized feedback for the individual and for the organization. When specific and relevant questions are asked, then specific and relevant solutions can be implemented.

Action Planning

THIS IS where the rubber meets the road. Now that you have assessed yourself and determined where you need to focus your improvement, it is time to create your action plan. To help you with this, we have included action plan worksheets in this book.

Your action plans will be more meaningful and effective if you draw from your assessments and the tips included in relevant sections. So before writing up your action plans, review all your assessments and the sections of *LEAD NOW!* that apply to the areas you want to improve.

Setting appropriate goals is often difficult. As you formulate your goal statements for each action plan, ask yourself these questions, which represent the essential elements of an appropriate goal.

- Is it realistic (challenging, but not too difficult)?

- Is it challenging enough (will it really push you to improve)?

- Is it measurable (do you know if you are progressing)?

- Is it dated (when will it be achieved)?

- Whom will you share it with? (Accountability is a key to achieving your goal.)

Guidelines on Completing the Individual Action Plan Template

An IAP helps provide you with purpose, dedication, and direction. It keeps the value of your feedback data current and meaningful by giving you the answer to "What do I do with all of this feedback data?" You are putting your data into *action*, which will create growth and a stronger impact for you, your relationships, your current role, and your life!

Having a plan and writing down the steps to achieve your goals is essential in creating sustained behavioral change. Below are instructions and tips on how to create an IAP. Following the five parts of the plan will help you build stronger leadership ability and establish support structures so you can achieve your development goals.

Part 1: Focus Statement

Your first step is to write a focus statement at the top of the action plan. You want to identify no more than one Leadership Dimension per action plan. We recommend one to two action plans at a time. Each action plan typically has a lifespan of three to four months. After that, you can revise or retire the action plan as you create a new one.

From your LEAD NOW! assessments, determine the area you wish to improve using the following recommendations:

- The more specific the statement, the more likely you are to be successful.

- Address your focus statement in behavioral terms rather than broad generalities.

- The more measurable your statement, the easier it will be to track your progress.

- Be realistic yet willing to challenge yourself as you write your statement.

- Remember, you will create more action plans after this, so avoid the tendency to work on everything at once.

- Be reasonable with yourself and take this process one step at a time.

- Include what the impact will be when you accomplish your goal.

Part 2: Action Steps

This section is the heart of the action plan: write out the specific steps to accomplish your focus statement. To accomplish real change, each step needs to be personal and specific to your current position and focus statement. You do not need to complete all ten of the rows provided. Do what works for you. Use the Coaching Tips for further insight and clarification.

In addition to the steps, decide on dates or milestones associated with each step under the By When column; setting a date or timeline will help keep you focused on your end goal. The third column, Who Helps?, is where you write the name of someone you trust to hold you to your commitment. As well as helping you with your action steps, this person becomes a part of your support system and provides you with resolve and accountability.

Part 3: Relevant Gems and Lessons

List the Gems and Lessons from the Stewart Leadership Series that are the most relevant in helping you achieve your focus statement. You can locate them using the *52 Gems* and *52 Lessons* books, where each Gem and each Lesson begins with its related Leadership Dimensions. Find the ones most closely associated with your focus statement and list them in this section. Refer to them often.

Part 4: Potential Barriers and Solutions to Those Barriers

List what and/or who are the potential barriers as you complete your IAP. Stating this allows you to plan ahead and anticipate any roadblocks that could get in the way of you completing your action steps. If there are barriers, who and/or what are the solutions that will address the barriers? For example, if you are called on a remote assignment for the next six weeks, what mitigating actions could you take to make sure your action plan stays alive and relevant?

Part 5: Support Signatures

The final part of the plan is to put teeth into your goal by asking your coach/support person and your boss to support you by signing your IAP. This requires them to read through your finished product and offer their encouragement and ongoing feedback.

Here is a checklist to use as you create your IAP:

1 Have I shared my IAP with my manager and incorporated their feedback?

2 How do I plan to discuss my IAP progress with my manager?

3 Do I address the skills I need to do my job now and those I'll need to achieve my career goals?

4 Do I have an appropriate mix of experiential, relational, and formal learning?

5 Will the successful outcome of my IAP help my organization and team?

6 Do I address both my strengths and opportunities?

7 Will my IAP push me out of my "comfort zone"?

8 Have I created achievable metrics to measure success?

9 Have I created milestones to keep me on track?

10 Who will support and follow up with me?

Action Plan
Templates

We have provided both a blank action plan and two filled-in sample action plans on the following pages. These demonstrate effective goal statements and focus areas.

Stewart Leadership Individual Action Plan—Template

Focus Statement

Briefly identify what area you wish to develop. This may be an area of strength or a gap. Consider what will be most helpful in achieving the desired business and people results for your organization and career.

_____

_____

_____

_____

_____

_____

_____

_____

_____

_____

_____

_____

_____

Rating of Focus Area

Identify how well you do this competence or behavior (on a 1–10 scale). This can be revisited throughout the coaching process to identify progress.

1 = Little/ No Competence	5 = Moderate Competence	10 = Excellent Competence
Date		
Rating		

Action Steps

Identify the steps or activities that will help you accomplish your focus statement. Draw from the LEAD NOW! Coaching Tips, Leadership Gems, and Leadership Lessons. Tailor your steps to fit your specific situation.

Steps	By When	Who Helps?
1		
2		
3		
4		
5		
6		
7		
8		
9		
10		

Resources

Identify a role model with whom you can observe/discuss your target behavior(s).

_____

Use these additional LEAD NOW! resources to support your action planning (consider using LEAD NOW! videos and LEAD NOW! coaching cards as well):

LEAD NOW! Coaching Tips
Dimension _____ in *LEAD NOW!* book

Leadership Gems (in *52 Leadership Gems: Practical and Quick Insights for Leading Others*)

\# _____

\# _____

(Pay particular attention to the reflection section at the end of each Gem chapter)

Leadership Lessons (in *52 Leadership Lessons: Timeless Stories for the Modern Leader*)

\# _____

\# _____

(Pay particular attention to the application section at the end of each Lesson chapter)

Barriers and Solutions

List what and/or who are the potential barriers, and who and/or what are the solutions to address these barriers as you attempt to complete your Individual Action Plan. Consider availability of budget, supplies, labor, time, attitude, industry factors, and support of management.

Potential Barriers	Solutions to Barriers
1	1
2	2
3	3

Individual Signature: _____

Date: _____

Support: _____

Date: _____

Boss: _____

Date: _____

Stewart Leadership Individual Action Plan—Examples

IAP Example 1: Effective Communication (Dimension 2)

Effective communication is the ability to express an intended message, through the best medium, in a manner that the recipient of the message will understand. It involves a willingness to repeat messages, incorporate others' feedback, and re-craft messages so that those involved are aligned and understand the communication. Consider the perspective of others and adjust the message and medium accordingly. Remember, the biggest hurdle to effective communication is the assumption that it has taken place.

Focus Statement

My people have told me that I can sometimes deliver mixed messages and don't always share information freely with them. Things move quickly and priorities can shift, but I know I need to do a better job of keeping my team "in the know" so they can manage priorities, feel empowered to solve their own challenges, and meet deadlines.

Action Steps

Identify the steps or activities that will help you accomplish your focus statement. Draw from the LEAD NOW! Coaching Tips, Leadership Gems, and Leadership Lessons. Tailor your steps to fit your specific situation.

Steps	By When	Who Helps?
1 Solicit feedback from trusted colleagues regarding their perception of my ability to communicate. Encourage them to be honest and complete in their observations.		
2 Ask a trusted colleague to sit in on one of my staff meetings, take notes, and review their notes with me in private.		
3 Ask my boss how they want to be kept informed (preferred style, method, frequency, quantity, etc.).		
4 Ask my team how they want to be informed (preferred style, method, frequency, quantity, etc.).		
5 On a Post-it Note, write a list of behaviors that I want to avoid as I lead meetings. Privately review this list immediately before entering a meeting.		
6 Write down the percentage of how often I communicate in person versus electronically. Ask my colleagues and boss if this is what they want.		
7 Select a trusted colleague with whom I will share this action plan. Ask them for support in monitoring my progress.		
8		
9		
10		

Resources

Identify a role model with whom you can observe/discuss your target behavior(s).

_____

Use these additional LEAD NOW! resources to support your action planning (consider using LEAD NOW! videos and LEAD NOW! coaching cards as well):

LEAD NOW! Coaching Tips
Dimension 2: Effective Communication in *LEAD NOW!* book

Gems (in *52 Leadership Gems: Practical and Quick Insights for Leading Others*)
#4: The Biggest Hurdle to Effective Communication Is the Assumption That It Has Taken Place

#50: Tell Them *Why*

(Pay particular attention to the five reflection statements at the end of each Gem section)

Lessons (in *52 Leadership Lessons: Timeless Stories for the Modern Leader*)
#17: Big Ears Are a Must

#49: Tuning In to Crickets

(Pay particular attention to the five application statements at the end of each Lesson section)

Barriers and Solutions

List what and/or who are the potential barriers, and who and/ or what are the solutions to address these barriers as you attempt to complete your Individual Action Plan.

Consider availability of budget, supplies, labor, time, attitude, industry factors, and support of management.

Potential Barriers	Solutions to Barriers
E.g., I'm in meetings so often that I don't have time to talk with my team.	E.g., Schedule time during the week so that I am available to answer questions from my team and provide them with the information they need.
1	1
2	2
3	3

Individual Signature: _____

Date: _____

Support: _____

Date: _____

Boss: _____

Date: _____

IAP Example 2: Delegating (Dimension 6)

Delegating is the ability to communicate a given task so that the individual assigned to it understands the objective and timeline, is provided available resources to complete the task, and knows you will support and not abandon or take over the task. Delegating is a demonstration of trust in your people that they and you can do more. Successful delegation requires a conscious choice to share the workload and let others learn and prove themselves.

Focus Statement

I often resist delegating assignments to others because I know I can do them better. It saves me time to just do the job. However, I recognize that I need to train my people on how to do certain tasks. I know that if I develop my ability to delegate, it will free up my time to be more strategic (something that will help me in my career progression) and develop my team members' skills to a greater degree.

Action Steps

Identify the steps or activities that will help you accomplish your focus statement. Draw from the LEAD NOW! Coaching Tips, Leadership Gems, and Leadership Lessons. Tailor your steps to fit your specific situation.

Steps	By When	Who Helps?
1 Have an individual conversation with each team member to learn how they prefer to be delegated to.		
2 When delegating a task, ask my people if they have the needed resources and support to accomplish their assigned tasks.		
3 Analyze what barriers arise in completing delegated tasks within my team.		
4 Create an accountability structure for completing the delegated task and assign an appointed time of when they will need to return and report.		
5 When delegating, tell the person why the task is important.		
6 Select a trusted colleague with whom I will share this action plan. Ask them for support in monitoring my progress.		
7		
8		
9		
10		

Resources

Identify a role model with whom you can observe/discuss your target behavior(s).

Use these additional LEAD NOW! resources to support your action planning (consider using LEAD NOW! videos and LEAD NOW! coaching cards as well):

LEAD NOW! Coaching Tips
Dimension 6: Delegating in *LEAD NOW!* book

Gems (in *52 Leadership Gems: Practical and Quick Insights for Leading Others*)
#42: Give Them the Ball and Let Them Run with It

#50: Tell Them *Why*

(Pay particular attention to the five reflection statements at the end of each Gem section)

Lessons (in *52 Leadership Lessons: Timeless Stories for the Modern Leader*)
#3: Employees Are Like Turtles

#47: Snake and Eggs

(Pay particular attention to the five application statements at the end of each Lesson section)

Barriers and Solutions

List what and/or who are the potential barriers, and who and/ or what are the solutions to address these barriers as you attempt to complete your Individual Action Plan. Consider availability of budget, supplies, labor, time, attitude, industry factors, and support of management.

Potential Barriers	Solutions to Barriers
E.g., I was just promoted over a new group and am unsure how each team member responds to delegated assignments.	E.g., Ask each person their delegation preferences and explain my expectations of delegated assignments.
1	1
2	2
3	3

Individual Signature: _____

Date: _____

Support: _____

Date: _____

Boss: _____

Date: _____

About the Authors

John Parker Stewart

John Parker Stewart is the founder and CEO of Stewart Leadership, which he started in 1980. He is globally recognized as a leadership coach, consultant, educator, speaker, and team performance specialist. Under his guidance, Stewart Leadership is recognized internationally for its feedback assessments, training tools, and solid, results-focused coaching services designed to guide teams and individuals to adapt, grow, and reach new levels of performance.

John has coached and trained tens of thousands of leaders worldwide including CEOs, presidents, military, government, and business leaders resulting in significant, measured improvement in individual and team performance.

John began his undergraduate studies at the University of Colorado, finished his bachelor's degree at Brigham Young University, and earned his master's degree in organizational communication where he wrote his thesis at Parliament in London. He began his doctoral work and teaching at Michigan State University, and continued doctoral studies under management guru Peter Drucker in executive performance and leadership at Claremont Graduate University.

John started his career managing leadership and management development for 86,000 employees at Lockheed Corporation. He was selected "National Trainer of the Year" by the American Society for Training & Development (ASTD). In addition to training and coaching all levels of management at Kennedy Space Center over an eight-year period during the high-pressure space shuttle program, John has worked with Citibank, Chevron, Lockheed Martin, Toshiba, CSL-Hong Kong, Xerox, GM, Kaiser Permanente, Telstra, US Department of Energy, Shell, and other government agencies and commercial firms.

John has published several articles, manuals, workbooks, and the three-book award-winning Stewart Leadership Series. The first edition of his title book, *LEAD NOW! A Personal Leadership Coaching Guide for Results-Driven Leaders*, won the National Indie Excellence Award for the best leadership book published over the last five years. His *52 Leadership Lessons* is also nationally recognized. John's latest book is titled *Mastering the Art of Oral Presentations*, published by John Wiley & Sons. This book is an essential tool for orals teams seeking to win government contracts, as well as a valuable guide for presenters in any field.

John lives with his wife, Debra, near Portland, Oregon, and has four sons and sixteen grandchildren.

Daniel J. Stewart

Daniel J. Stewart is a sought-after talent management and leadership development consultant and coach with proven experience advising senior leaders, leading change, and designing leadership-rich organizations. He leads Stewart Leadership's extensive consulting practice, business development, and international partnerships.

Over the past twenty years, he has been an internal and external organizational development executive and consultant delivering talent and team development solutions, executive leadership coaching, group facilitation, change management, organizational design, and strategic planning for JetBlue Airways, Briggs & Stratton, Avaya, University of Wisconsin–Milwaukee, Lockheed Martin, The Weihs Group (venture capital), Kohl's department stores, and Aurora Health Care, among others.

He is the co-author of *LEAD NOW! A Personal Leadership Coaching Guide for Results-Driven Leaders*, which was awarded first place by the National Indie Excellence Awards for best leadership book published over the last five years. He has also published articles in *Executive Excellence, Practicing OD, Proposal Management*, and HR.com.

Daniel is originally from California and Oregon and lives near Milwaukee, Wisconsin, with his wife, Katie, and their four children.